LAS CRUCES
TRADITION, PROSPERITY, FUTURE

GEORGE PINTAR

Las Cruces—Tradition, Prosperity, & Future is a historical fiction work ©Copyright by George Pintar December 2024. Names, characters, businesses, organizations, places, events, and incidents either are the product of the author's imagination or are used fictitiously. Any resemblance to an actual person, living or dead, occurrences, or locals is coincidental.

All rights reserved. Las Cruces--Paradise, Published in the United States by KDP, a division of Amazon, Inc.

Library of Congress cataloging-in-publication data is on file with the Library of Congress.

First edition December 2024

Design Cover by a KDP

ISBN:9798304894867

DEDICATION

This book is dedicated to the past, present, and future Las Cruces City Councils and city employees, including Policemen, Firefighters, and Librarians.

> "As a rule, what is out of sight
> Disturbs men's minds more
> Seriously than what they see."
> ---Julius Caesar, Gallic War (58 – 51 B.C.)

ACKNOWLEDGMENTS

I want to thank some of those who have helped me over time. First, thanks to Maryann Costa, who co-edited this book, and Liz Vega, Jan Thomas, and Paul Mathews.

Thanks to Mary Holguin, my caregiver, who takes care of the house and meals while I toil at my computer. I apologize to my wife, Jean, who supported my endeavors without complaining.

I am grateful for the privilege of living in the Land of Enchantment. The stimulating atmosphere created by all those exceptional and unusual human beings who inhabit it constantly inspires me and not only assists me in this book but also encourages me to want to do many more.

TABLE OF CONTENTS

ROOTS OF LAS CRUCES TRADITIONS

Introduction of the Characters……………….Page 1

The Battle of Growth……………………......Page 18

Romance in the Air…………………….…..Page 34

The Breaking Point…………………….…...Page 42

Resolution…………………………………….…..Page 51

Resilience…………………………………….Page 56

CHAPTER ONE
The Transition of Las Cruces……………..Page 65

CHAPTER TWO
Continuing to Change……………….……..Page 78

CHAPTER THREE
Seeds of Transition……………………….…Page 111

CHAPTER FOUR
Conclusions and Prospects……………….Page 118

CHAPTER FIVE
Steps to the Future of Las Cruces………..Page 140

CHAPTER SIX
Vision for Las Cruces's Future…………….Page 153

ROOTS OF LAS CRUCES TRADITIONS

INTRODUCTION OF CHARACTERS

From the late 1800s to the early 1900s, Las Cruces, New Mexico, was on the brink of a thrilling transformation. As it approached statehood in 1912, it embodied the rugged yet hopeful spirit of the Southwest. The town's unique character, a rich tradition woven from Hispanic, Anglo, and Native American cultures, was evident in the thick, sundried walls of the adobe buildings that dotted the landscape.

The streets, a blend of dusty trails and newly carved roads, bustled with the steady rhythm of horse-drawn wagons, the bleating of livestock, and the hum of voices from merchants, farmers, and travelers alike as children ran alongside wagons.

Las Cruces was on the cusp of a remarkable transformation, where each footstep, hoofbeat, and wheel turn hinted at the promise of progress. Shopkeepers haggled with customers, and the scent of freshly turned earth mingled with leather and hay, painting a vivid picture of a community ready to evolve from its rugged beginnings into a bustling hub of trade and industry.

This period marked a significant trade, transportation, and communication boom, as the railroad and telegraph's arrival was pivotal in Las Cruces' history. It brought an influx of settlers, merchants, and opportunity.

Railroad tracks extended through the arid landscape, linking it to larger markets and making it a vital trade hub for agricultural goods, cattle, and local artisanship.

The railroad and telegraph were the catalysts for the town's growth. New businesses and saloons sprang up around the railway station, their swinging doors opening to farmers, ranchers, and railway workers eager to exchange goods, stories, and news from far-off places.

With the promise of growth, however, came tension and challenge. Land disputes, remnants of territorial conflicts, and cultural clashes occasionally simmered in the desert heat.

Mexican, Anglo, and Indigenous influences were deeply woven into the town's fabric. Yet, pressure from Anglo settlers and the heated discussions of statehood shifted the social dynamics, redefining property rights and community leadership. These years of rapid change also saw the rise of reform movements, church missions, and educational initiatives as the community traversed the balance between preserving its traditions and embracing new opportunities.

Las Cruces, a testament to its community's toughness, emerged as a town where neighbors stood together through droughts, challenging harvests, and conflicts over land and identity.

The town's adobe structures and Chile-drying ristras hanging from wooden beams cast a colorful picture, reminders of an old and evolving legacy. By the time New Mexico attained statehood in 1912, Las Cruces was no longer a remote village but a flourishing town, its roots grounded in a past of hardships and its branches reaching toward a new, unified future as part of the United States.

▲▲▲▲▲

Maria Elena Chavez was a resilient woman of mixed Spanish and Native descent, rooted deeply in her heritage and the land her family had cultivated for generations near the Rio Grande River. Her ancestors were among the early settlers, building a life along the river that nourished the land and their traditions. Maria Elena's days were filled with the rugged demands of ranch work — from mending fences to tending livestock — but she saw these chores as a form of stewardship, honoring her ancestors' sacrifices and sustaining the land they cherished.

Maria Elena Chavez, in her mid-forties, carried a quiet elegance that stood out amid the rugged New Mexico landscape. Her skin was sun-kissed and weathered from the years under the intense desert sun, giving her a naturally bronzed glow. Strands of silver weaved through her dark, thick hair, which she often pulled back loosely, allowing a few wisps to frame her robust and expressive face. Her eyes were warm and sharp, holding the steady gaze of someone who had witnessed and endured much.

Though softened by time, her features were strikingly handsome, with high cheekbones and a faint, almost mischievous smile that spoke of strength and silent wisdom. Maria Elena's attire was practical yet graceful, often in muted earth tones that blended seamlessly with her surroundings. She moved with purpose and quiet confidence, embodying an elegant strength that only deepened with age.

She was keenly attuned to the natural world's rhythms, guided by the wisdom passed down through her family. As her father grew older, Maria Elena took on more responsibilities, balancing modern ranching practices with the knowledge her family had preserved.

She was a robust and quiet force within her community, admired for her tireless work ethic and unwavering connection to the land that sustained her people. Her hands bore the strength of a lifetime of toil, yet her touch was tender when nurturing the gardens, livestock, and traditions passed down through generations. She embodied the spirit of her heritage, honoring the wisdom of her ancestors while inspiring those around her with a profound sense of resilience and purpose. Whether offering sage advice, helping, or simply leading by example, her presence was a steady beacon of pride and unity in the community.

Outside her work, Maria Elena was also known for her skills in traditional crafts, like weaving and pottery, which she learned from her grandmother. Each piece she created told a story of her lineage, symbolizing the blend of Spanish and Native influences that shaped her life.

Locals highly valued her work, and she shared these traditions with the younger generations, hoping to instill the same respect for her deeply felt heritage. For Maria Elena, every piece of land, every crafted object, and every moment spent on the ranch spoke to the enduring bond between her people and the land they called home.

▲▲▲▲▲

Samuel Blake arrived in Las Cruces with little more than his well-worn cavalry coat and a silent resolve for peace. A former Union soldier from the rolling hills of Tennessee, he carried a quiet dignity that masked the burdens of war. Standing tall but unassuming, Samuel sought solace in this new town, far from the divided lands he'd known.

He was a ruggedly handsome man in his late forties, exuding calm confidence from years of life experience. His physique was lean and athletic, with the toned, wiry build of someone who maintained their fitness through regular outdoor activities. His broad shoulders and solid, steady posture gave him an air of quiet strength. His face was angular, with high cheekbones and a squared jawline softened by a hint of laugh lines around his eyes and mouth.

Samuel's hair was dark with streaks of early gray, cut neatly but often tousled, as if he spent a lot of time outdoors. His piercing eyes were a steel blue, sharp and observant, yet they held a warmth that put others at ease. He had a neatly trimmed beard flecked with gray, adding a touch of maturity to his otherwise youthful appearance. His sun-kissed skin showed a faint, weathered texture, a testament to the years he'd spent on the battlefield.

Samuel's style was practical and unpretentious. He wore functional, slightly worn clothing—often jeans, sturdy boots, and a simple button-down shirt. Whether leading a discussion or simply listening, he carried himself with a natural authority and a warm openness that made him approachable to all. Still, his gaze also had an undeniable hint of mystery, as though he'd seen and experienced more than he ever let on.

He was drawn to the vastness of the desert air and rugged mountains, which were unlike anything he'd ever seen. Samuel marveled at the blend of Mexican, Anglo, and Native American traditions that shaped Las Cruces, each culture adding its thread to the fabric of the town's identity. He learned about their customs and toughness while engaging in respectful conversations.

It wasn't long before Samuel opened a modest store stocked with essentials and a few luxuries—a business that allowed him to meet townsfolk from all occupations. As he settled into his role as a merchant, he quickly earned a reputation for his fairness and quiet wisdom. Those who came to him for supplies often left with more than they'd bargained for—a few calm words of advice or a steady reminder of neighborly goodwill.

Samuel became a natural mediator, always finding a path through conflict and reminding people of common ground when disputes heated up.

Over time, people came to see Samuel as a fixture in the community—a man who listened without judgment and whose words carried the weight of experience. Still healing from the Civil War's divides, he is a rare bridge who understands the toll of conflict and the price of peace. Though he rarely spoke of his past, Samuel carried the scars of his journey with quiet strength.

▲▲▲▲▲

Don Fernando Ortega — A prominent and powerful figure in Las Cruces, Ortega was a wealthy landowner and shrewd businessman with a vast network of connections. Known for controlling a large share of the region's trade, Ortega built his fortune through calculated investments and, at times, hard-nosed tactics.

He was a man shaped by the rugged land and fiery sunsets of the desert, with eyes still carrying the intense spark of youth despite his fifty-some years. His skin, weathered and bronzed, spoke of long days spent under the sun while deep lines carved his face, a testament to years of grit, laughter, and anger that burned hot beneath the surface. When Don Fernando spoke, his voice rumbled low, like distant thunder, but his words could bite with the sharpness of a desert rattlesnake, quick to lash out when his temper flared.

Whiskey was his warm companion, a comfort that fueled his fire and tempered his solitude. He took a sip and sighed, savoring each drop as if it held memories of love, loss, and the dusty trails of his life. Beneath the bravado was a shadow, a hint of vulnerability he kept hidden. For Don Fernando, whiskey was more than a drink; its ritual reminded him that even the most robust flames need fuel to keep burning.

Driven by an unyielding ambition to see Las Cruces flourish, Don Fernando tirelessly championed the development of new railroad and telegraph lines, viewing them as the region's lifeblood for trade and growth. With each new track or pole added, he envisioned greater commerce and a transformed city, connected to the broader economy and bustling with opportunity.

To him, these railways and telegraph lines were more than infrastructure—they were the foundation of his legacy as a visionary city builder who foresaw a thriving future and refused to rest until Las Cruces claimed its place as a commercial hub in the Southwest.

However, his aggressive pursuit of influence and profit was not without consequences. Many local ranchers and farmers viewed his methods as overbearing, if not ruthless. Don Fernando's strong-arm tactics often involved pressuring smaller landowners and monopolizing critical resources, increasing resentment among those who felt displaced or marginalized by his growing empire.

Tensions simmered as he battled to gain control over crucial land parcels essential for the railroad and telegraph expansion, clashing with those who held fast to their traditional livelihoods. While admired for his business acumen, Don Fernando's unyielding quest for dominance divided Las Cruces, with some seeing him as a visionary and others as a man willing to sacrifice community for personal gain.

▲▲▲▲▲

Toh-Nah — A young Tortugas man from the Piro-Manso-Tiwa tribe and a spiritual guide, he carried the weight of his people's history and persistent challenges. Having witnessed firsthand the erosion of Tortugas land and traditions under U.S. government policies, he felt a profound responsibility to protect and sustain the wisdom, customs, and spiritual practices passed down through generations.

His life was woven with the teachings of his ancestors, and he approached each day with an awareness of his role as a bridge between the past and present. This dedication to preserving ancestral knowledge was not just a duty but a personal mission he upheld with reverence and care, ensuring that these traditions remained meaningful for future generations. His commitment shined through in every ritual he performed, every story he told, and every lesson he imparted to those willing to listen.

As a Tortugas warrior honed by years of endurance and discipline, his frame was powerful but not overly imposing. He was built for agility as much as strength, and his muscles were defined and lean like a panther's. His skin was sun-bronzed, etched with faint scars that told of battles fought and hardships overcome. High cheekbones and a strong jawline frame his face, which often rested in quiet contemplation, though his piercing dark eyes revealed a depth of thought and wisdom far beyond his years.

Emotionally, Ton-Nah exuded a quiet strength and natural authority. His words, though few, were carefully chosen, resonating with the weight of experience and a connection to traditions passed down through generations. He carried the burdens of his people and the land with a quiet resolve balanced by a compassion that tempered his fierceness.

Ton-Nah's wisdom flowed from an intimate knowledge of nature, the rhythms of the earth, and the lessons of both joy and suffering. His presence was calming and inspiring, as he guided others with a steady hand, encouraging those around him to find their strength and spirit. Those who sought his counsel felt humbled and uplifted, knowing they were in the presence of someone who had looked deeply into life's mysteries and emerged unshaken.

Ton-Nah walked a delicate path: while outwardly complying with imposed regulations, he tirelessly and quietly preserved his people's culture. Skilled in storytelling, ceremony, and traditional knowledge, he became a mentor to the younger generation, instilling pride amidst the pressures to assimilate.

His journey was one of unwavering resilience, shaped by a fierce commitment to honor the spirits of the land and uphold his ancestors' legacy. In the face of relentless challenges and constant external and internal threats, he never faltered. With each step, he carried the weight of generations before him, striving to protect the sacred traditions that had sustained his people for centuries.

The land, steeped in history and alive with ancestral significance, beckoned to him with an ancient and profound voice. It called upon him not merely as a protector but as a devoted steward, urging him to embrace a role of reverence and preservation. This was no mere obligation of survival; it was a sacred pact—a recognition of the interconnectedness of past, present, and future, etched into the soil and whispered through the wind.

Throughout his journey, he navigated treacherous physical and spiritual paths, constantly tested by forces that sought to strip away his heritage and displace his community. But his resolve was more potent than any obstacle. The memory of his forebears fueled his determination, and the wisdom of the elders whispered to him in moments of doubt. He was more than a guardian;

he was a bridge between the past and the future, a living testament to the strength and perseverance of his people.

The threats became more insidious as the years passed, but his spirit remained unbroken. Whether facing colonial encroachment, political upheaval, or the erosion of cultural practices, he found innovative ways to protect his heritage while adapting to the changing world. His journey was not just about survival—it was about thriving, ensuring that the land's spirits and the stories of his ancestors would continue to guide future generations.

Ultimately, his commitment became a leader for others, inspiring those who shared his vision and carrying the flame of resistance forward. His legacy would be endurance and transformation—proof that resilience is a response to adversity and a declaration of life's enduring power in the fight to preserve identity.

THE BATTLE OF GROWTH

Maria Elena Chavez was a passionate advocate for her community, navigating the challenges posed by rapid development in the region. The influx of new residents and businesses significantly changed the once close-knit area, and many conflicts deeply concerned Maria Elena.

One of her primary struggles was preserving the area's cultural heritage, a legacy rooted in centuries-old traditions and community ties. Rapid urbanization threatened to erase the land's rich history, replacing adobe homes and family-run farms with high-rise buildings and sprawling subdivisions. Maria Elena worked tirelessly to raise awareness about the importance of cultural preservation, organizing town hall meetings, collaborating with local historians, and petitioning local governments to designate historical sites for protection.

Another critical issue was the loss of agricultural land. Commercial developments and asphalt roads replaced the fertile fields that once sustained generations of farmers. Maria Elena understood the economic pressures driving this shift but fought to balance growth and sustainability. She formed alliances with local farmers and environmental groups, advocating for policies supporting agricultural preservation, such as tax incentives for family farms and urban planning initiatives prioritizing green spaces.

Beyond these tangible issues, Maria Elena faced the intangible yet pervasive challenge of uniting a community increasingly divided by economic disparity and shifting demographics. She worked to bridge the gap between long-time residents and newcomers, fostering dialogue and encouraging inclusive initiatives that respected the area's traditions while embracing the innovation potential.

Maria Elena's efforts were not without resistance. Developers and some local officials viewed her as an obstacle to progress, while others questioned the practicality of her vision. Yet, she remained steadfast, driven by a deep love for her community and a belief that growth did not have to come at the expense of heritage and harmony.

Through her advocacy, Maria Elena Chavez became a symbol of resilience, a voice for those who sought to protect their roots while navigating the future. Her legacy inspires a new generation of community leaders striving to achieve a sustainable and inclusive balance in an ever-changing world.

As Las Cruces expanded, many residents voiced concerns over the gradual loss of traditional farming practices and the encroachment of development on ancestral lands. Maria Elena Chavez stood at the forefront of this battle with her unwavering commitment.

The fertile soil along the Rio Grande, which had supported generations of farmers, began to give way to new housing and businesses. However, with their resilience, the community continued to define the area, even in the face of such changes.

Local farmers worried about the impact of reduced farmland on crop yields and the region's self-sufficiency. Others raised alarms about the depletion of water resources and natural habitats. However, as the sprawl continued, the emergence of sustainable development policies brought hope for preserving the area's agricultural legacy and natural heritage.

Several initiatives emerged, like community-supported agriculture programs, farmer's markets, and conservation easements. These were designed to protect farming traditions and create a bridge between Las Cruces' rural past and its future.

Maria Elena Chavez was particularly vocal about preserving Las Cruces's cultural identity, advocating for protecting local traditions and farmers' rights. This put her at odds with Don Fernando Ortega, other developers, and city planners who prioritized growth and economic development, often at the expense of community values and environmental sustainability.

Additionally, she faced challenges in rallying support from the community, as differing opinions on development priorities often led to divisions among residents. Her efforts to advocate for a more sustainable and culturally sensitive approach to development highlighted the broader struggles between modernization and preserving community heritage during this period of change in Las Cruces.

Samuel Blake had a keen eye for opportunity and a heart full of dreams. A sharp-eyed, reserved newcomer, he quickly became known for his practicality and fairness. Samuel's store was a gathering place for locals, a hub where news, supplies, and stories were exchanged, and the community came together.

As he walked the bustling farmer's market with its vibrant colors and scents, he spotted Maria Elena. She was a spirited woman with a warm smile and a fierce sense of independence. They initiated a conversation, instantly bonding over their shared experiences in this tight-knit community. With her deep appreciation for the rugged landscape surrounding them, Maria Elena spoke passionately about the desert's beauty and the resilience it inspired in its inhabitants.

He found himself at the center of the town's dynamics, often balancing Don Fernando's powerful influence and agenda against the needs of the independent ranchers and farmers who relied on his store for their supplies.

As Samuel and Maria Elena's friendship blossomed, they frequently met at the market, sharing stories and dreams. Maria Elena often encouraged Samuel to stand firm against Don Fernando's manipulations, urging him to prioritize the ranchers' welfare over profit.

Together, they navigated the complexities of life in Las Cruces, their bond strengthening as they faced challenges in a town where loyalty and survival were intertwined.

Samuel's understanding of the profound community ties in Las Cruces deepened through his friendship with Maria Elena. He realized that every transaction at his store was a business deal, a chance to support his neighbors and foster a collective spirit of resilience. Samuel found a kindred spirit in Maria Elena, who shared his struggles and his love for their shared home, the land of Las Cruces.

As time went on, Samuel became not just a merchant but a key player in shaping the town's future. He always strived to balance the competing interests of power and independence and found strength in the friendship that anchored him in a world of uncertainty.

He met Don Fernando Ortega, whose roots run deep into the rugged landscape. Though their personalities clash—Samuel is guarded and meticulous, Don Fernando is more outspoken and unrestrained—their shared status fosters a loose but enduring friendship. Both men share a mutual respect for the land and a certain solitude, feeling out of place among the town's old-timers and independent ranchers who hold sway over local matters.

As Samuel's store grows in importance, he becomes an unintentional mediator between Don Fernando's influence, which can be both fiery and divisive, and the ranchers' needs. Don Fernando's strong personality often puts him at odds with the ranchers, who value their independence and don't appreciate interference.

Although sympathetic to Don Fernando, Samuel strove to maintain a delicate balance. He knew that his place in the town depended on navigating its tangled web of alliances. He carefully weighed each decision, knowing that even a hint of favoritism could ripple through the town's social fabric, affecting his standing and the community's stability.

His loyalty to Don Fernando didn't run deep, yet he understood the importance of diplomacy in a town where alliances shift as quickly as desert sands. Samuel's steady composure and calculated neutrality were his shields, allowing him to tread the fine line between support and impartiality.

Over time, Samuel's role became pivotal as a storekeeper and a link between the town's rugged characters. Each day brought new challenges, as he found himself caught between Don Fernando's ambitions and the demands of the ranchers. All while trying to keep his store afloat amid the changing tides of the town's shifting loyalties, not to mention his concern about Maria Elena.

Toh-Nah joined Samuel at his store, his weathered face lined with concern, eyes scanning the familiar faces of ranchers and villagers gathered around. His voice, steady but urgent, warned them of the railroad and telegraph's looming impact—their threat not only to the land they've tended for generations but also to the delicate balance of the local wildlife that called this place home. He spoke of the buffalo herds, once so plentiful but now dwindling, and the river whose waters may soon be diverted or polluted by the construction.

They promised progress and wealth, yet Toh-Nah saw the cost—the inevitable scars on the land and the disruption of age-old patterns that have sustained both people and animals.

As he spoke, some nodded in agreement, while others shifted uneasily, caught between the promise of opportunity and the loss of the world they knew. Samuel listened, too, his gaze fixed on Toh-Nah, recognizing the wisdom in his words and the urgency in his tone.

With each step, Toh-Nah felt the weight of his ancestors' voices, urging him to protect the sacred lands from the steady encroachment of iron rails and smokestacks. His deep-rooted commitment to preserving the land was clear, yet he faced a struggle that seemed increasingly impossible, pitted against powerful forces that valued profit over preservation.

As Toh-Nah spoke to the gathered ranchers and villagers, his voice was calm but carried an urgency that resonated with Maria Elena, who watched him from the crowd. She understood his plight all too well. Her family's land, stretching across open fields and forested groves, had been threatened as developers eyed the region for expansion.

Maria Elena sensed a bond with Toh-Nah, a shared recognition of their families' sacrifices to safeguard their heritage. She felt compelled to stand by him, knowing that the fight to protect their lands is as much about preserving their way of life as it is about defending the fragile ecosystems that depend on it.

The two joined forces, rallying others in the village to see the importance of conservation over progress at any cost. Together, Toh-Nah and Maria Elena drew upon both traditional knowledge and the practical concerns of the ranchers and villagers, hoping to spark a resistance that could protect the land from the railroad's relentless advance. They knew the battle would not be easy, but with each step, they solidified their determination to guard what remained of their ancestral lands, hoping their voices would be loud enough to be effective before it was too late.

Toh-Nah's presence was a quiet but powerful reminder of his people's deep bond with the land. He spoke solemnly to the ranchers and villagers, urging them to understand the railroad's inevitable encroachment and destructive impact on the environment and local wildlife. Toh-Nah's words echo a warning of what's to come: loss of habitat for animals, contamination of water sources, and the gradual erasure of the land his ancestors walked, lived, and depended upon.

He faced resistance from those enticed by the railroad's promises of economic growth and those simply unable to comprehend the long-term effects on the ecosystem. Every plea and conversation felt like a fight, with Toh-Nah struggling against a tide of development that valued profit over preservation. His resolve to protect the land never wavered, but he grew weary as he witnessed ancient forests marked for clearing and rivers redirected.

Among the villagers, Maria Elena was among the few who understood Toh-Nah's struggle. Her family's land stood on the edge of change; its future was threatened by encroaching industries eager to exploit resources. She had seen her family's way of life steadily undermined and knew that, like Toh-Nah, they were fighting an uphill battle.

Maria Elena and Toh-Nah share an unspoken understanding, a bond formed from mutual loss and a fierce, protective love for their ancestral lands. Together, they rally others, gathering those will listen to their cause and instilling a sense of duty to safeguard their heritage. Despite the formidable odds stacked against them, their unwavering commitment to protecting the land deepened.

Together, they cultivated a sense of community, inspiring others to join their mission. Their collective efforts addressed immediate challenges and paved the way for innovative solutions, ensuring that future generations would inherit a thriving planet.

Don Fernando, the powerful landowner in the region, exerted immense pressure on Maria Elena's family to sell their ancestral land, a tract rich in cultural heritage and agricultural potential. His influence extended deeply into the local government, allowing him to manipulate land use to serve his interests.

Historically, landowners like Don Fernando often leveraged their connections with town officials to marginalize smaller landholders, a tactic rooted in the legacy of land distribution injustices that had plagued the region since the early 20th century.

As tensions rose, Samuel, a community mediator and ally of Maria Elena's family, sought a peaceful resolution. He aimed to engage both parties in dialogue, highlighting the importance of family heritage and the community's agricultural legacy.

However, he quickly faced formidable obstacles. Don Fernando's allies, entrenched within the local political framework, closed ranks against Samuel's efforts, employing intimidation tactics to dissuade dissent.

Maria Elena's family stood firm in its refusal to sell, drawing strength from generations of forebearers who worked the land and preserved their cultural identity. Yet, as their defiance grew, so did the harassment from Ortega's men, who hired thugs to conduct Don Fernando's bidding.

These men, encouraged by the landowner's support, escalated their campaign of intimidation, making it clear that Maria Elena's family's commitment to their land would come at a steep price.

The situation reflected a broader historical narrative of land disputes in the region, where families often found themselves caught between powerful interests and their right to maintain their homes and heritage. As Maria Elena's family continued to resist, the stakes became higher, not just for their future but for the very fabric of their community.

ROMANCE IN THE AIR

Over the following weeks, Samuel became a regular at Maria's home, often stopping by for his morning coffee and a pastry. Each encounter was laced with playful banter and lingering glances, the chemistry between them palpable. Maria looked forward to his visits, her heart fluttering at the thought of seeing him.

One afternoon, as the sun dipped low in the sky, casting a golden hue over the town, Samuel mustered the courage to ask Maria if she would join him for a walk in the nearby park. The moment was electric, filled with anticipation. They shared stories of their lives, dreams, and aspirations as they strolled under the blossoming trees.

Laughter rang out around them, creating a joyful symphony that made the rest of the world fade into the background. At that moment, it was as if time stood still, leaving just the two of them enveloped in their little bubble of connection. The warmth of their shared laughter drew them closer, deepening their bond and allowing them to forget everything else. They felt a sense of belonging in that serene space where nothing else mattered but the joy of being together.

As they passed by a small pond, Samuel gently brushed a loose strand of hair behind Maria's ear, his fingers grazing her cheek. Time stood still, and in that tender moment, the air thick with unspoken feelings, Maria felt a warmth spreading through her, a realization that this was the beginning of something beautiful.

Samuel leaned in, their eyes locking in an intimate gaze filled with unspoken emotions. As their lips met in a soft, tentative kiss, a spark ignited between them, sealing the promise of a blossoming romance that would change their lives forever. Time seemed to stand still as the world around them faded away, leaving only the warmth of their connection.

The kiss was gentle yet electric, a delicate exploration of their feelings' depth. It lingered, leaving them breathless and momentarily suspended in time. Before this, their courtship had been a series of understated yet deeply meaningful gestures.

They had spent countless evenings strolling through moonlit paths, their footsteps crunching against the gravel in perfect harmony. Each walk was accompanied by the quiet symphony of rustling leaves and whispered stories of their pasts. They shared laughter over simple picnics by the lake, where the golden sunlight danced on rippling water, casting a dreamy glow around them. Their conversations blended with the gentle whispers of the breeze, filling the air with warmth and connection. As they both reached for the same slice of ripe, juicy peach, their fingertips met, sending a spark that made their hearts race. Caught in the moment, their eyes locked, and a tender smile spread across their faces. Slowly, they leaned in, their lips meeting in a deep, passionate kiss that seemed to stop time, leaving only the sweetness of love in its wake.

On rainy afternoons, they lingered in bookstores, pointing out passages that resonated with their hearts, often exchanging shy glances over the tops of well-worn pages. They had planted a small garden together, hands brushing through the soil as they tucked seeds into the earth, dreaming aloud about the flowers that would bloom in time.

It wasn't in grand ballrooms but under the stars' soft light, barefoot in the dew-kissed grass when they danced. Their laughter was the only music they needed as they spun each other in playful circles. And when words weren't enough, they turned to simple acts of care—folding each other's favorite blanket, brewing a cup of tea just the way the other liked, or leaving notes with little reminders of affection tucked into unexpected places.

With every heartbeat, they felt the weight of their pasts begin to lift, shedding burdens they had carried for far too long. It wasn't an abrupt release but a gradual unraveling, like the slow dissolution of clouds after a storm. In its place, a sense of renewal bloomed, making room for the endless possibilities that stretched ahead like an uncharted horizon.

Their kisses weren't just the culmination of these moments; they were unspoken promises — vows not uttered in words but deeply felt, resonating in the shared rhythm of their breaths. They spoke of trust earned and an imagined future where their lives, now inextricably intertwined, would be enriched by the quiet yet profound intimacies they could only share.

The world around them faded; its once insistent noise dulled to a soft hum. Time seemed to pause, holding its breath as if the universe recognized this exchange's significance. In that stillness, they were no longer individuals bound by their histories, but a single entity defined by hope and the beauty of connection.

Their entwined hands tightened just slightly, a small but powerful gesture affirming what words could never fully capture: a love that promised to transform, heal, and endure.

However, amid the bustling adaptation to unfamiliar customs, forming lasting connections felt secondary to navigating the uncharted challenges of this evolving world. These shifts brought uncertainty and a focus on survival, making marriage seem impractical, if not entirely out of reach for them.

▲▲▲▲▲

Toh-Nah contemplated his next move as he stood at the edge of the vast landscape he has always cherished, now marred by relentless modernization. A storm brewed within him as he contemplated more drastic measures to protect what remained of his home. The weight of his ancestors' spirits pressed upon him, urging him to take a stand. In a moment of clarity, he resolved to approach Maria Elena and Samuel, knowing their shared passion for the land and its future.

He found them at their usual meeting spot, a weathered oak tree that had withstood the test of time, much like their friendship. Toh-Nah laid out his bold plan to sabotage a key railway line, the lifeblood of the encroaching industry, which threatened to devastate their environment further.

"This is not just about protest; it's about survival," he insisted, his voice steady but tinged with urgency.

He hoped their alliance, forged through years of shared struggle, would give his plan the strength it needed.

As Maria Elena and Samuel listened, their expressions reflected concern and determination. Maria Elena's brow furrowed, contemplating the potential consequences of such an action.

"We risk everything, Toh-Nah," she warned, her heart heavy with the thought of repercussions. Samuel, ever the pragmatist, suggested alternatives but recognized the desperation in Toh-Nah's eyes. Together, they weighed the gravity of the decision before them, understanding that their choice could be a turning point in the fight for their land and future.

At that moment, they realized that the battle ahead would require more than words; it would demand courage and sacrifice. With a solemn nod, they agreed to Toh-Nah's plan, each fueled by a fierce commitment to protect the land they hold dear.

The stakes were high, but the three's resolve was unbreakable as they prepared to act against the encroaching threat. Each carried the weight of their past experiences, drawing strength from shared hardships that had forged an unshakeable bond.

Samuel took the lead with his keen instincts and strategic mind, analyzing the landscape for potential weaknesses in their adversary's approach. Though gentle and cautious, Maria Elena channeled her quiet determination, ready to harness her agility to evade danger and protect her companions.

Meanwhile, Toh-Nah, the most fiercely brave of the trio, found a spark of courage within himself. Together, they strategized, their hearts coordinated as they prepared to confront the looming shadow threatening their sanctuary.

THE BREAKING POINT

Don Fernando caught wind of the impending plan to disrupt the railroad line. He decided to act first to separate Maria Elena, Samuel, and Toh-Nah from the community. He planned to burn the community building and blame Maria Elena.

His plan to sabotage unfolded on a chilly autumn night. A member of his followers was motivated by resentment and a desire to create a rift between the townspeople and Maria Elena's family.

Under the dim glow of the streetlamps, the saboteur stealthily approached the community center, a beloved gathering place for the townspeople. This building symbolized unity and warmth, making it an ideal target to convey a message of intimidation. As the clock struck midnight, the figure slipped into the shadows, carrying a small container filled with flammable liquid and a few incendiary devices designed to cause minimal structural damage.

Using a small cloth, the saboteur fashioned a wick and carefully placed it inside the container, ensuring it was well-hidden yet accessible. With swift, deliberate movements, he set the container against the side of the building where it was least visible but likely to catch the wooden siding ablaze. The figure lit the wick and retreated, vanishing into the night as flames flickered to life.

The fire caught hold, producing thick, acrid smoke that billowed into the night sky. The flames danced hungrily, crackling and popping, but the intent was not to destroy the building entirely but to send a chilling message that instilled fear and suspicion among the townsfolk.

The damage was visible by dawn: charred siding and broken windows mar the community center, starkly contrasting its previous state. As the townspeople gathered, whispers rippled through the crowd. Fear settled like a fog, and tensions rose. The community center, once a sanctuary, now symbolized vulnerability.

Don Fernando, sensing an opportunity, stepped into the chaos. He stood on the steps of the charred building, addressing the crowd with a mix of outrage and calculated manipulation. "This is the result of Maria Elena and her family's influence on our town!" he declared, his voice ringing fervently. "They've brought danger to our doorstep! Are we to let them endanger our homes and our children?"

His words struck a chord. Already on edge from the incident, the townspeople turned their fear into suspicion and hostility toward Maria

Elena and her family. Don Fernando's strategy worked; he leveraged the fear of the unknown to rally support for his cause, framing Maria Elena as a scapegoat.

As neighbors glanced at one another with worry and distrust, Maria Elena and her family found themselves isolated, their once-friendly faces now turned cold by the fire of Don Fernando's rhetoric. Though limited in scope, the planned sabotage ignited a wildfire of fear and division within the town, leaving lasting scars on the community and escalating tensions that threatened to boil over.

Don Fernando and Maria Elena stood face to face on the weathered front porch of Samuel Blake's store, the creak of the loose wooden boards beneath their feet punctuating the charged silence.

"You can't deny it, Maria Elena!" Don Fernando's voice was sharp, his finger jabbing toward her. "You've always had a temper, and now look what you've done—our community building is gone! Do you have any idea what you've destroyed?"

Maria Elena crossed her arms, her chin held high. "Don't you dare, Fernando," she retorted, her tone as cold as the winter wind sweeping through the dusty street. "I wasn't near the community building last night, and you know it."

"The community building was more than just wood and nails!" Fernando shouted, his voice thick with anger and grief. "It was the heart of this town. A place where families gathered, weddings were celebrated, and we held the town meetings that you always had so much to say!"

Maria Elena's expression softened briefly but quickly masked it with defiance. "And you think I would burn it down? The same place where I organized the charity bake sales and taught the kids how to dance during Fiesta week? You're delusional, Fernando."

"You've been against expansion from the start," he shot back. "Many people heard you arguing with Mr. Greaves about the new plans. Isn't it convenient that the fire breaks out right after your latest tantrum?"

Maria Elena took a step closer, her eyes blazing. "A tantrum? You're so quick to point your fingers, Fernando. Maybe it's because you're trying to hide something. Or someone."

His face reddened. "What are you implying?"

"I'm not implying anything," she said with an icy smile. "I'm saying it outright: You have as much to gain from this disaster as anyone. Maybe more. Weren't you the one saying the old building was too run-down to fix and that we'd be better off with something new and shiny, funded by your out-of-town investors?"

Behind them, the door to the store swung open with a thud, and Samuel Blake stepped out, his gray brows furrowed. "That's enough, both of you," he barked. "This isn't the place for your accusations."

Maria Elena didn't budge, her gaze locked on Fernando. "Fine," she said coolly. "But mark my words, the truth will come out. And when it does, I'll be the one standing tall."

Don Fernando clenched his jaw, his voice dropping to a low growl. "We'll see about that."

Across the street, smoke still curled faintly from the blackened remains of the community building, a stark reminder of the loss. Once proud and sturdy, the frame was now a skeleton of charred beams, the scorched bell from the tower lying in the ashes. The smell of burned wood and memories hung in the air; a bitter scent stung the nose and the heart.

The nearby locals shook their heads in disbelief, murmurs carrying across the gathering.

"She can't be serious," muttered an older man with a weathered face, arms crossed tightly over his chest.

"Serious or not, she's got a point," countered a younger woman, her tone sharp as she gestured toward the commotion.

"Point or no point, someone's bound to get hurt if this keeps up," another voice chimed in, heavy with concern.

The crowd continued to buzz with speculation, each voice adding a layer of tension to the charged atmosphere.

The community was divided as discord among the townspeople became increasingly disillusioned with Don Fernando's oppressive rule. Many saw him as a self-serving leader who wanted growth at any price.

Now Maria Elena, Samuel, and Toh-Nah emerged as resistance advocates, embodying a defiant hope that inspired their neighbors.

Toh-Nah, an enthusiastic community organizer, sensed the simmering unrest. He rallied people from neighboring villages, organizing protests with the energy of those long unheard. Each protest grew, and more villagers joined in, igniting a movement that defied the danger Don Fernando's power presented.

Maria Elena's family's resolve became a powerful testament to the spirit of resistance, stirring a community divided by fear to unite in the face of tyranny. Neighbors quietly brought food and water to their homes, showing solidarity. Though frightened, people took pride in their resilience, finding strength in each other and believing that change was possible and within reach.

RESOLUTION

The showdown was about to begin. In a tense final confrontation, Ortega's carefully woven plans unraveled. Maria Elena, Samuel, and Toh-Nah, armed with damning evidence of Ortega's corruption, stood before the townspeople to expose his underhanded dealings.

The townsfolk, long suspicious of Don Fernando's questionable practices, were stunned by the proof of his bribery, land theft, and manipulation. A murmur grew among the crowd as Maria Elena, Samuel, and Toh-Nah revealed each heart-wrenching detail.

Voices began to overlap, some shouting, others whispering, yet all united in a genuine demand for accountability and change. People exchanged determined glances, and fists tightened, each person feeling the weight of the story Samuel and Maria Elena shared. Powerful energy filled the air, an unspoken vow they would not leave until the truth was known and justice was served.

Don Fernando tried to defend himself, but his words faltered, and the weight of his misdeeds became undeniable. Local authorities, once intimidated by his influence, now moved forward with his arrest, finally stripping him of the power he'd wielded unjustly for so long.

▲▲▲▲▲

With Don Fernando Ortega's departure, Las Cruces felt relieved and liberated from his oppressive influence. In his absence, a renewed spirit of unity emerged among the people who had long yearned for a chance to rebuild their community. Neighbors who once walked in fear now gathered in the plaza, sharing stories of struggle and survival and celebrating the newfound freedom that filled the air.

Local artists and musicians returned to the streets, bringing life back to the city with murals of hope and songs of resilience. Small businesses flourished, and community leaders rose to guide Las Cruces through its rebirth, fostering collaboration and trust that had been stifled for so long.

Traditions once threatened under Ortega's rule were revived with fierce pride as the people of Las Cruces reclaimed their city and their identity.

Empowered by this victory, the townsfolk banded together to restore fairness and community values, paving the way for a brighter, more harmonious future.

Maria Elena and Samuel embarked on a new chapter in Las Cruces, each bringing their skills and passions to enrich their community. Samuel took on a pivotal role, working closely with town leaders, local businesses, and residents to shape a more balanced and sustainable path for the town's development.

He championed community-centered planning, ensuring that growth respected the area's heritage and met the needs of future generations. Samuel gained the community's trust through his thoughtful approach, guiding them to embrace ideas that honor tradition and progress.

Meanwhile, Maria Elena found renewed confidence in her role at the family ranch, blending old practices with innovative methods. She oversaw the ranch's daily operations, cultivating the land with respect for her family's legacy and a commitment to sustainable ranching.

Maria Elena strengthened her ties with the local agricultural community, forming alliances and participating in programs that supported ranchers facing challenges in an evolving industry. Her dedication inspired others, and her ranch became a model of resilience and respect for the land.

Toh-Nah quietly but effectively emerged as a respected leader and advocate for Indigenous rights and environmental preservation. Working within and beyond the community, Toh-Nah protected Indigenous land, customs, and language. He collaborated with organizations that preserved sacred spaces, shared his knowledge of cultural history, and advocated for policies that respected Indigenous heritage.

Toh-Nah's commitment resonated deeply within his community, and he became a voice for the traditions and values he held dear, ensuring they continued to thrive for future generations.

Samuel, Maria Elena, and Toh-Nah built a foundation of mutual respect, personal growth, and a shared vision of hope for the future in Las Cruces. Together, they cultivated a space where cultural traditions and progressive ideas merged harmoniously, creating opportunities for meaningful connections.

Their efforts extended beyond their close-knit circle, influencing others in the community to embrace collaboration and understanding. With his steadfast determination and open-minded approach, Samuel worked tirelessly to bring people together.

Maria Elena's warmth and wisdom became a guiding light, inspiring those around her to see the potential in every individual. Meanwhile, Toh-Nah, grounded in heritage and a deep connection to the land, shared stories and practices that reminded everyone of the importance of unity and balance.

Their collective efforts enriched their lives and left an enduring legacy in Las Cruces, where respect, growth, and hope became cornerstones of a thriving and inclusive community.

RESILIENCE

Community bonds ran deep in Las Cruces, strengthened by a shared history of resilience and a collective determination to protect the land and heritage that defined their way of life. This deep commitment shined through as residents united to honor and safeguard their cultural traditions, natural environment, and collective identity.

Through local gatherings, festivals, and conservation initiatives, they actively preserved their heritage, passing down stories, values, and practices from generation to generation. Whether revitalizing historical landmarks, advocating for sustainable practices to protect their surroundings, or celebrating cultural events that defined their community's spirit, the residents stood united.

This dedication strengthened their bonds and shaped a resilient community that honors its past while looking confidently toward the future. From local farmers safeguarding their agricultural land to neighborhoods advocating for sustainable development, the people of Las Cruces demonstrated steadfast dedication to maintaining their unique landscape and culture.

Family values, respect for cultural diversity, and a profound appreciation for the natural beauty of the Chihuahuan Desert were embedded in the community's daily life. Festivals like the Whole Enchilada and the Dia de Los Muertos united the community, reinforcing their shared love for their traditions and environment.

Inspired by the desert's colors and textures, local artists and artisans brought cultural expression to life in murals, pottery, and textiles lined the streets and markets, representing the community's identity.

In facing challenges like rapid urban development and environmental issues, Las Cruces residents united through grassroots organizations and public forums, showing remarkable tenacity in protecting their surroundings. Initiatives to conserve water, promote local businesses, and support green spaces reflected a forward-looking approach, ensuring that future generations would inherit a community that thrived from its natural and cultural wealth.

The city's adobe architecture and historic Mesilla Plaza reminded residents and visitors alike of its storied past, while new businesses, universities, and technology hubs represented a vision for the future. Las Cruces's warmth and pride were evident in every neighborhood as they embraced sustainable growth, invested in green spaces, and fostered a connection that bridged generations. Through this dedication, Las Cruces continued to thrive as a place of both heart and progress, forever honoring its cultural roots.

The combination of the Tortugas Tribe, Spanish, and Anglo Cultures made Las Cruces a unique challenge to coexistence. A rich tapestry was woven from the threads of the three traditions, each bringing its language, beliefs, customs, and historical roots. This blend created a multi-layered society visible in every aspect of life, from architecture and art to food, music, and festivals.

However, these cultures faced unique challenges as they navigated their shared space, each striving to preserve their heritage and identity in a rapidly changing world.

Tortugas reservation residents maintained deep spiritual and ancestral connections to the land, central to their identities and lifeways. Yet, they often confronted pressures from modernization, land rights disputes, and a complex relationship with city, state, and federal governments.

Spanish traditions, dating back over four hundred years, remained firm, with customs and languages passed down through generations. However, as Las Cruces grew and diversified, Hispanic culture also needed to find ways to adapt without losing its core.

▲▲▲▲▲

The arrival of Anglo settlers in the 19th century added another dimension, bringing Western ideologies, industrial advancements, and new governance structures. While Anglos contributed to the economic and infrastructural development of Las Cruces, this influence had sometimes overshadowed and disrupted Indigenous and

Hispanic traditions, leading to tensions and cultural misunderstandings.

These groups continued to find ways to coexist, celebrate, and learn from one another. Intercultural dialogue and collaborative art and history projects emerged to bridge gaps, promote mutual respect, and honor the diversity that defined Las Cruces. This blend of cultures, while challenging, was also a testament to toughness and the shared desire for understanding, unity, and the preservation of their heritage.

The railroad and telegraph's arrival transformed the landscape, bringing promise and peril. For local communities, it symbolized a decisive struggle between the forces of progress and the desire to preserve cultural and natural heritage. As the tracks extended across previously untouched lands, the railroad opened new opportunities for trade and communication, connecting distant towns and expanding the reach of commerce.

However, this expansion came at an inflated cost to local ecosystems and traditional ways of life. Trees were cleared, disrupting habitats and forcing wildlife to adapt or perish. Rivers were diverted, altering natural water flows that had sustained biodiversity for centuries.

Lands that had supported generations of families were irrevocably altered, leaving fields barren. These changes eroded the environment and severed cultural ties to the land, leaving scars etched into the landscape.

For some, the railroad and telegraph represented the future—a gateway to prosperity and modernization. Near the rail line, Las Cruces experienced rapid growth, and businesses flourished, creating jobs and economic advantages.

But for others, the relentless push for development threatened the very essence of their identity. The railroad brought an influx of settlers and new land use, encroaching on historical and spiritual significance.

The local population grappled with this change, caught between embracing new opportunities and mourning the loss of their ancestral connections to the land. The clash between advancing technology and cultural preservation became a defining theme that still resonates in discussions about land, progress, and heritage.

This complexity examined how justice found its way into situations through the unlikely alliances among diverse populations. As each pursued goals and faced struggles, their paths intertwined, leading them to realize they shared a greater purpose.

Through collaboration, they exposed hidden truths, sought justice for past wrongs, and confronted their biases, gradually uncovering more profound layers of systemic injustice. Everyone brought their unique perspective, challenging preconceived notions and enriching their collective understanding. As they engaged in difficult conversations, they dismantled long-standing barriers, fostering empathy and trust. Over time, their efforts transformed into a movement that acknowledged the wounds of the past and advocated for long-lasting change. United with a shared sense of responsibility, they forged a path to creating a more inclusive and equitable future for all.

Each alliance was forged not from common backgrounds but from a shared determination to make things right. United to challenge a flawed system, whether from different social classes, cultures, or even opposing sides of the conflict, redemption was often a collective journey.

At its core, it conveyed a message of hope, underscoring that a better future was possible when people came together, transcending their differences and past mistakes, to create lasting change. Las Cruces's history was a blend of toughness, diverse cultural influences, and a community spirit that had shaped its unique heritage.

▲▲▲▲▲

Founded in 1849, Las Cruces began as a modest agricultural settlement nestled along the fertile banks of the Rio Grande. Its rich alluvial soil and favorable climate quickly drew farmers and ranchers eager to cultivate the land. Initially, settlers planted traditional grain crops, mirroring the agricultural practices of the East. However, they soon discovered that the unique environment of the Southwest called for adaptation.

The region's arid conditions and intense sunlight proved challenging for some grains, but they provided ideal conditions for other crops like Chile peppers, pecans, and cotton. These became staples of the local economy, shaping Las Cruces's agricultural identity. Over time, innovative irrigation techniques and the ingenuity of its farmers transformed the area into a thriving hub for Southwestern agriculture.

As settlers diversified their crops, they developed a strong community centered on shared labor and traditions. They blended Eastern practices with the cultural influences of nearby Indigenous and Mexican populations, creating a unique heritage that continues to define the character of Las Cruces today.

The town's name, meaning "The Crosses" in Spanish, was steeped in local legend—some say it refers to the grave markers for travelers who perished along El Camino Real. In real contrast, others believed it commemorated a tragic massacre of Spanish settlers in the early days of colonization.

With New Mexico's statehood in 1912, Las Cruces emerged as an inspiration for progress in the Mesilla Valley. It embraced innovations in agriculture and trade while preserving its deep-rooted traditions.

During the latter part of the 20th century, Las Cruces experienced another wave of growth by establishing New Mexico State University, expanding the nearby White Sands Missile Range, and developing Spaceport America. These institutions brought intellectual diversity and economic stability, drawing residents from all occupations.

Las Cruces was proud of its past and forward-looking ambitions. Its story was one of adaptation and unity, a testament to the many people who had contributed to its growth over the centuries. The history of Las Cruces wasn't merely one of dates and events; it was a legacy of enduring strength shaped by the people who called it home.

This unique intersection of cultures and traditions continues to shape Las Cruces, creating a dynamic community where the past and present converge seamlessly. The city's rich tapestry of influences—ranging from Native American roots to Spanish and Mexican heritage and the contributions of newer residents—fosters an environment where diversity is celebrated.

This fusion empowers individuals to honor their heritage and grow in a space that values collaboration and shared experiences. Local festivals, markets, and artistic endeavors reflect this harmonious blend, allowing residents and visitors to connect with the region's cultural heartbeat.

The enduring sense of belonging that defines Las Cruces inspires its people to take pride in their unique identity, nurturing a community that thrives on unity, creativity, and mutual respect. Whether through preserving traditions or embracing innovation, the spirit of Las Cruces remains firmly rooted in the belief that its strength lies in its rich cultural crossroads.

CHAPTER ONE

The Transition of Las Cruces

The evolution of Las Cruces from an agrarian society to a modern, technology-driven city reflects its ability to adapt and thrive amidst rapid change. Initially centered around agriculture, particularly in the fertile Mesilla Valley, where crops like Chile peppers, pecans, and cotton flourished, the city sustained a community that relied on the region's natural resources.

This agrarian foundation laid a solid cultural and economic groundwork, where farming families and agricultural businesses contributed to a tight-knit, self-sufficient community. As technological advancements transformed the global economy, Las Cruces began to shift away from a purely agrarian identity, gradually embracing innovation in various sectors. The New Mexico State University was pivotal in fostering educational growth and attracting researchers, scientists, and entrepreneurs to the area.

The university evolved into a center for agricultural research, driving innovation in local farming techniques and fostering a sustainable approach to agriculture. By seamlessly blending traditional methods with modern scientific practices, it not only enhanced crop yields and resource management but also served as a model for ecological stewardship. This transformation brought together experts, students, and local farmers in collaborative initiatives, creating a dynamic environment for experimenting with new technologies, such as precision agriculture and regenerative farming. The university's outreach programs further strengthened its impact, offering workshops, demonstrations, and community partnerships that empowered farmers to adopt more resilient and environmentally conscious practices.

The next phase of growth came with the rise of the aerospace and defense industries. The proximity to White Sands Missile Range and other federal research installations drew significant government and private-sector investment, creating new job opportunities and stimulating the local economy. These industries brought in highly skilled workers, elevating the city's profile as a scientific and technological innovation hub.

In recent years, the shift toward information technology and remote work has further redefined the Las Cruces economy. Digital infrastructure improvements have allowed the city to attract IT companies, software developers, and tech startups. Initiatives to support tech education and entrepreneurship have empowered a new generation of local innovators.

Coworking spaces are shared work environments where individuals and small or large groups from different organizations or professions work independently or collaboratively. These spaces are designed to foster productivity, creativity, and networking by providing resources and amenities such as desks, meeting rooms, high-speed internet, and communal areas.

Coworking spaces cater to freelancers, remote workers, small business owners, startups, and corporate teams, offering flexibility through membership plans or pay-as-you-go options. They emphasize a sense of community and often host events, workshops, and networking opportunities to enhance professional connections among members. Incubators have also sprung up, enabling small businesses and freelancers to thrive alongside established companies. Additionally, the city's appeal has grown among telecommuters, who are drawn to Las Cruces for its affordable living, scenic beauty, and cultural life.

Today, Las Cruces exemplifies a blend of the old and new. Its agrarian roots remain an important cultural touchstone, while the city's embrace of information technology, science, and innovation speaks to its resilience and forward-thinking spirit. As Las Cruces grows, its evolution is a testament to how a city can adapt, diversify, and thrive in the modern age.

The rise of the information and technology sector significantly stimulated population growth in Las Cruces beginning in the early 2000s. This expansion was fueled by the city's strategic location, proximity to research institutions like New Mexico State University, and initiatives to attract tech companies. Establishing technology parks and increased investment in infrastructure created job opportunities, drawing a diverse workforce to the area.

As startups and established firms flourished, Las Cruces became a regional hub for innovation, particularly in sectors like aerospace, renewable energy, and software development. The tech boom reshaped the economic landscape and spurred the development of housing, schools, and cultural amenities to accommodate the growing population. By the end of 2024, Las Cruces had cemented its reputation as a dynamic city blending technological progress with a rich cultural heritage.

As Las Cruces continues through the 21st century, it experienced a transformative wave of technological growth and digital connectivity that reshaped its economy, education, and community dynamics—this period marked the beginning of a digital era in the city, with advancements in internet infrastructure that have supported the growth of modern businesses, startups, and a thriving local tech scene.

The 21st century saw the introduction of advanced irrigation techniques to optimize water usage. These innovations in water management were crucial for conserving water resources and supporting sustainable farming in arid regions.

Farmers began shifting their crop selections to adapt to changing climate conditions and evolving market demands. This diversification helped strengthen agricultural resilience and improved profitability by aligning production with consumer needs.

Adopting machinery in farming revolutionized the agricultural landscape, marking a pivotal shift toward modernized practices. Mechanization increased efficiency, reduced labor demands, and empowered farmers to manage larger plots of land with greater precision. Innovations such as mechanical reapers, seed drills, and steam-powered tractors enabled a transition from subsistence farming to large-scale agricultural enterprises. This transformation significantly boosted productivity, allowing for higher yields and meeting the growing demands of expanding populations.

Additionally, mechanization reduced the physical toll on laborers and diversified the agricultural workforce, as fewer individuals were required for manual tasks. However, this shift also brought challenges, such as the initial machinery cost, the need for specialized skills to operate and maintain equipment, and the displacement of traditional farm laborers. Despite these hurdles, the long-term benefits of mechanization laid the foundation for sustainable, scalable farming and reshaped the rural economy, fostering growth and innovation in the agricultural sector.

Expanding internet access and installing broadband networks have played a pivotal role in modernizing the Las Cruces economy. In 2024, significant investments in telecommunications infrastructure transformed the city, enabling high-speed internet access to businesses, educational institutions, and residential neighborhoods. These advancements bridged the digital divide and positioned Las Cruces as a competitive hub for technology-driven industries, remote work opportunities, and innovation. Enhanced connectivity has empowered local entrepreneurs, attracted new businesses, and improved access to education and telehealth services, further bolstering the city's economic resilience and growth potential.

This connectivity has been instrumental in helping local businesses adopt e-commerce and digital marketing, allowing them to reach broader markets and stay competitive in the digital age. As a result, many small businesses and startups have emerged, leveraging technology to innovate in fields such as agriculture, tourism, and retail.

In recent years, Las Cruces has adopted several "smart city" initiatives to improve the quality of life through technology. The city has embraced technology to enhance public services and environmental sustainability, from energy-efficient street lighting to intelligent traffic management systems. Public Wi-Fi zones in parks and community centers, along with digital kiosks, make information more accessible, allowing residents and visitors to benefit from the city's connectivity.

The city council's "smart city" initiatives, which used technology and data, were designed to improve the quality of life for its citizens and the efficiency of city services.

The expansion of digital connectivity has directly impacted the educational system and workforce development and has also profoundly impacted education in Las Cruces. New Mexico

State University's local community colleges have been able to offer more online programs and distance learning options, catering to non-traditional students and working adults.

Partnerships with technology companies have introduced coding boot camps, workforce development programs, and job training in software development, cybersecurity, and data analytics, helping cultivate a tech-savvy workforce prepared to support the region's evolving economy.

Recognizing the importance of equitable access to technology, Las Cruces has implemented digital inclusion initiatives to close the digital divide. Programs offering discounted internet service, free public computer labs, and digital literacy training ensure that residents of all ages and backgrounds can benefit from the city's digital transformation.

CHAPTER TWO

Taking Shape

Las Cruces, the second-largest city, is a hidden gem in southern New Mexico. The city's history, shaped by Hispanic, Anglo, and Native American influences, is woven into every aspect of life here — from its distinctive adobe architecture to its lively festivals and world-class cuisine.

This blend of cultures gives Las Cruces a rare and unforgettable character, offering a rich tapestry of traditions, art, cuisine, and history. From its picturesque landscapes, framed by the Organ Mountains, to its thriving local markets and festivals celebrating its diverse heritage, Las Cruces is a must-visit destination for anyone seeking the Southwest's beauty, flavor, and spirit. Whether you're exploring the historic Mesilla Plaza, indulging in its renowned green Chile dishes, or enjoying the warm hospitality of its residents, Las Cruces invites visitors to immerse themselves in a truly exceptional cultural experience.

Hispanic traditions are rich with dazzling festivals, music, and culinary flavors that reflect Spanish-speaking communities' diversity and cultural heritage worldwide. These traditions provide a sense of joy and celebration, strengthen family bonds, and uphold community values passed down through generations, like Maria Elena's.

Festivals such as *Dia de los Muertos, Cinco de Mayo, and Festival of Our Lady of Guadalupe Tortugas* are integral to Hispanic culture. These festivals are filled with colorful parades, traditional dances, and food, creating an atmosphere of unity and celebration. They offer an opportunity for families to come together, paying homage to their cultural roots while embracing modern influences.

Music is another cornerstone of Hispanic traditions, with genres like salsa, merengue, flamenco, and mariachi playing a central role in bringing people together. These rhythms and melodies express joy and passion, preserve history, and tell stories of struggle, love, and triumph. Whether it's the lively beats of a salsa band or the heartfelt lyrics of a ranchera, music unites people across generations and geographical boundaries.

Culinary traditions in Hispanic cultures are deeply rooted in family and community, serving as a vital connection between generations and celebrating shared heritage. Foods like Enchiladas, red or green, Gorditas, or Chile Rellenos take center stage at gatherings, from festive holidays to simple Sunday meals, fostering a sense of belonging and unity. Also, iconic dishes such as tamales, empanadas, pozole, and arroz con pollo are lovingly prepared, often involving multiple family members.

Grandmothers, mothers, and aunts are the guardians of these treasured recipes, which are meticulously passed down through oral traditions or handwritten notes. Each dish carries the imprint of time-honored techniques, regional influences, and personal touches, creating a tapestry of flavors unique to each family.

Preparing tamales, for instance, is often a communal affair. The extended family gathers to spread masa on corn husks, fill them with savory or sweet ingredients, and steam them to perfection. This shared labor becomes a joyful event filled with storytelling, laughter, and the strengthening of familial bonds.

These culinary practices are about sustenance, preserving identity, and expressing love. Meals are imbued with symbolism, whether the welcoming aroma of freshly baked pan dulce signals comfort or the meticulous assembly of an altar laden with traditional foods during Día de los Muertos, which honors ancestors.

In Hispanic cultures, food is more than nourishment—it is a bridge between the past and present, a celebration of life, and a testament to the enduring power of community and tradition.

Beyond festivals and food, Hispanic traditions emphasize values such as respect for elders, a strong sense of family, and community solidarity. These values are taught from a young age, with children learning the importance of looking out for one another and taking pride in their heritage. Hispanic cultures continue to thrive and evolve through these customs while maintaining a deep respect for their history and the bonds that keep families and communities together.

▲▲▲▲▲

European settler's influence contributed to architectural styles like Western art, creating a fusion of modern and traditional aesthetics. Blending rich histories with modern perspectives creates a dynamic environment that fosters growth, mutual respect, and shared prosperity.

This harmonious collaboration encourages individuals to celebrate their unique backgrounds and embrace the collective strength of diverse experiences. Together, they understand that these differences are not obstacles but valuable assets enriching their shared journey.

Recognizing the power of diversity, they strengthen the bonds that unite them, building a foundation for a future where unity, creativity, and inclusion are living, thriving realities across generations. By nurturing this inclusive spirit, locals inspire innovation and cultivate a sense of belonging, ensuring every voice is heard, and everyone can contribute to a brighter, more interconnected tomorrow.

▲▲▲▲▲

European incomers did not begin settling in Las Cruces until after the conclusion of the

Mexican-American War in 1848, signaling a new era for the region. Soon after, pioneers started cultivating the fertile soils of the Mesilla Valley, drawn by its agricultural potential and proximity to the Rio Grande River.

Las Cruces quickly grew in prominence, becoming a vital stop along the historic El Camino Real de Tierra Adentro. This trade route connected Mexico City to northern outposts in New Mexico and beyond, facilitating commerce and serving as a cultural exchange conduit blending Spanish, Mexican, and Indigenous groups.

Las Cruces translates to "The Crosses" in Spanish and is steeped in melancholy history. According to legend, it originates from the crosses erected to mark the graves of settlers killed during encounters with Apache warriors who fiercely defended their ancestral lands. These memorials became a haunting reminder of the dangers early settlers faced while carving out a new life in the untamed frontier.

Las Cruces embraces its storied past while looking toward the future. Its rich history is preserved in its historic districts and landmarks, like the downtown Plaza de Las Cruces and Mesilla, where visitors can step back in time and experience the blending of traditions that shaped this resilient community.

Milestones in recorded Las Cruces history include the opening of the Rio Grande Theater, which showed silent movies in 1926. Three years later, the Great Depression set in, making financial success difficult.

There were better times intermingled with hardship in Las Cruces's history. The Women's Improvement Association established the first city library in 1924. A decade later, Alice Branigan funded a new library in memory of her husband, Captain Thomas Branigan. It was the only privately funded construction project conducted during the Great Depression.

The historic Branigan building became the Branigan Cultural Center, one of four museums operated by the city, and is now listed on the National Register of Historic Places.

Agriculture has been vital to Las Cruces. Fabian Garcia, a member of the first graduating class of New Mexico College of Agriculture and Mechanic Arts, now New Mexico State University, became director of the college's experimental station. He began testing crops that would benefit farmers transitioning away from grains. He is responsible for developing Chile peppers in New Mexico. He also brought strains of Acala cotton and the Grando sweet onion.

The railroad and telegraph's arrival in Las Cruces brought much excitement and profoundly transformed the city, sparking tensions among its residents. For some, they symbolized progress, economic opportunity, and a new era of connectivity. It also promised to put Las Cruces on the map as a hub of commerce and transportation, access to goods, faster communication, and the possibility of prosperity for merchants, ranchers, and farmers eager to send their products to distant markets.

Yet, many people—particularly small business owners and farmers—were deeply resistant to these changes. They disrupted traditional economies, making it difficult for local businesses and farmers to compete with the influx of cheaper, mass-produced goods. Long-established trade routes that relied on wagons and pack animals were quickly overshadowed by the speed and efficiency of the new transportation systems, leaving many without their livelihoods and struggling to adapt.

There were fears about the cultural impact. The railroad brought an influx of newcomers, including laborers, settlers, and entrepreneurs, which led to concerns about the dilution of local traditions and values. Some saw the rapid growth as a threat to the town's identity, while others worried about rising crime rates and lawlessness that sometimes accompanied boomtown expansion.

Tensions also rose between landowners and railroad companies. Their tracks often cut through private property, leading to disputes over compensation and rights-of-way. Ranchers were particularly frustrated as the rail lines disrupted grazing lands and sometimes divided herds. Economic development and growth clashed with the slower, rural pace of life many residents had known for generations.

Despite the challenges of adapting to innovative technologies, the disruptions caused by the railroad and telegraph undeniably shaped the future of Las Cruces. Over time, the town learned to leverage these technologies, turning its newfound connections into a gateway for growth and commerce in the Southwest.

However, they remain a poignant reminder of the struggle between embracing progress and preserving the town's historical identity. As modernization reshaped the landscape, long-standing traditions and ways of life faced gradual erosion. For some, this transformation signaled opportunity and growth, a chance to redefine their community and participate in the broader sweep of contemporary advancements. For others, it represented a bittersweet loss as the familiar rhythms of daily life and the cherished heritage that had defined generations began to fade into memory.

The juxtaposition of progress and preservation continues to echo in the town's architecture, festivals, and even its cuisine, where remnants of the past coalesce with the present innovations. It's a reminder that while change is inevitable, the values and stories of those who came before are worth safeguarding, ensuring they remain a guiding light for future generations.

▲▲▲▲▲

Some of the historical figures who roamed the streets of this region include Billy the Kid, the infamous outlaw and folk hero; a young Douglas MacArthur, who would later become a celebrated general; Kit Carson, the legendary frontiersman and scout; Roy Bean, the self-proclaimed "Law West of the Pecos"; the prominent Perez family, Lieutenant Colonel William Rynerson who was involved in law, mining, the railroad and local politics Albert Fountain, a prominent attorney and politician whose mysterious disappearance remains unsolved; Albert Fall, the controversial Secretary of the Interior implicated in the Teapot Dome Scandal; and Pancho Villa, the revolutionary leader whose raids brought international attention to the area. Martin Amado and his family were huge in the history of Las Cruces.

These individuals left an indelible mark on the history and folklore of the American Southwest. Their stories, filled with adventure, ambition, and often conflict, intertwine with the rugged landscape, creating a rich and enduring tapestry of history. From daring explorations to fierce battles and passionate struggles for power, these narratives are shaped by the land and its people. The challenges posed by untamed wilderness, harsh climates, and unyielding terrain serve as a backdrop to the pursuit of dreams and survival.

These tales, passed down through generations, continue to captivate historians, storytellers, and those seeking to understand the complexities of human nature. Whether recounted around campfires, woven into the fabric of ancient cultures, or dissected in academic circles, their influence endures, shedding light on timeless themes of morality, conflict, and the human condition.

Their intricate plots and rich symbolism resonate across Las Cruces's diverse societies, transcending time and geography. These mythic and historical stories inspire awe, provoke reflection, and invite us to question our values and beliefs. Their legacy remains an ideal long after the dust has settled, guiding future generations to pursue wisdom and understanding.

▲▲▲▲▲

Las Cruces has fully embraced the rapid population increase, positioning itself as a forward-thinking hub in the Southwest. Over the past fifty years, the city has experienced remarkable growth, doubling its population from fifty thousand to one hundred thousand. This transformation reflects its appeal as a place to live and its adaptability to emerging industries and technologies.

Integrating cutting-edge innovations into various sectors has revitalized the local economy, significantly benefiting agriculture, aerospace, and healthcare industries. Advanced systems are optimizing water use in farming, streamlining manufacturing processes, and improving patient care at medical facilities. The city's proactive approach to adopting these technologies has made it an attractive destination for tech startups and established companies.

As Las Cruces grows, it invests heavily in its infrastructure and workforce development. The local university and community college have introduced specialized programs to train residents in AI-related fields, ensuring a skilled labor pool that meets the demands of modern industries. Additionally, the city fosters collaboration through initiatives like tech incubators and innovation hubs, creating opportunities for entrepreneurs to thrive.

Las Cruces is a beacon of resilience and innovation in the Southwest with its strong sense of community, picturesque desert landscapes, and a forward-thinking commitment to technological progress. The city boasts a unique blend of cultural heritage rooted in its rich Native American,

Hispanic, and Anglo influences, creating a tapestry of traditions, art, and cuisine. Its stunning surroundings, including the Organ Mountains and the expansive Chihuahuan Desert, provide a haven for outdoor enthusiasts and inspire a deep connection to nature.

Las Cruces is not just looking to preserve its past but poised for a future of transformative growth. Investments in renewable energy, education, and small business development highlight the city's embrace of cutting-edge advancements while maintaining its small-town charm. The region's thriving agricultural sector, famous for producing world-class Chile, continues to innovate with sustainable practices, ensuring long-term prosperity.

As a hub for aerospace innovation, thanks to its proximity to Spaceport America, Las Cruces has positioned itself as a pivotal player in the next frontier of exploration. Combined with a burgeoning arts scene, inclusive public spaces, and a community-driven spirit, the city offers a dynamic and welcoming environment, attracting new residents, visitors, and businesses.

Las Cruces is more than a place to live — it's a place to grow, dream, and create. With its eyes firmly on the horizon, the city is well-prepared to embrace the challenges and opportunities of the coming decades, ensuring a bright and prosperous future for all.

With the promise of burgeoning economic opportunities and the arrival of new residents and businesses, the region is poised for a transformative decade. Experts anticipate a significant population surge fueled by strategic infrastructure, technology, and community development investments. This growth has brought hope and optimism, as it is expected to create a strong economy, diverse cultural opportunities, and improved quality of life for current and future residents.

However, with this anticipated growth comes a critical challenge—water. As Las Cruces and the surrounding region prepare to support a larger community, the limited water supply presents a potential bottleneck for sustainable development.

Las Cruces is already experiencing the tangible effects of climate change, which have significantly altered the region's weather patterns and environmental conditions. Over the past one hundred years, the average temperature in Las Cruces has increased by approximately 1°F, and this warming trend is expected to intensify in the coming decades. As a result, the city is anticipated to face more days with temperatures surpassing 105°F during the summer months, contributing to extended heatwaves and an increase in extreme temperature events.

In addition to rising temperatures, Las Cruces is witnessing more frequent and severe droughts, which considerably stress water resources, agriculture, and ecosystems. Shifting precipitation patterns further exacerbate these drought conditions, leading to more prolonged dry spells. The impact of these changes is evident in the increasing risk of wildfires. Las Cruces's homes and business buildings are at risk of wildfire, highlighting the city's vulnerability to these devastating events fueled by higher temperatures and drier conditions.

Another alarming consequence of climate change in Las Cruces is the growing frequency of flash floods. Due to rising temperatures and changes in storm patterns, the city expects more periodic flash floods, which cause significant property damage and strain local infrastructure. Furthermore, as snowpacks in nearby mountains shrink and melt earlier in the year, stream flows decrease, reducing water availability during critical summer months.

Dust storms, another climate-related phenomenon, are becoming more common in the region. The combination of higher temperatures, reduced vegetation, and soil degradation has made Las Cruces more susceptible to these dust storms, which can negatively affect air quality and public health. Additionally, the high temperatures, low humidity, and increased vapor pressure deficit associated with climate change increase ozone levels, contributing to smog formation. This increase in smog poses a significant health risk, particularly for vulnerable populations such as children, older people, and those with respiratory conditions.

Las Cruces faces various climate-related challenges, from extreme heat and droughts to wildfires, flash floods, and air quality issues. Addressing these challenges requires concerted efforts to reduce emissions, adapt to changing conditions, and build resilience in a rapidly changing climate.

Efforts are underway to explore innovative water conservation strategies, including advancements in water-efficient technology, intelligent irrigation systems, and sustainable agricultural practices. Significant investments are being made in modern infrastructure, such as upgrading pipelines to reduce leaks, implementing water recycling systems, and developing reservoirs to capture and store rainwater.

Fostering community awareness and engagement in water resource management is equally essential. Public outreach programs, educational workshops, and incentives for reducing household water consumption are helping to empower individuals and businesses to adopt more sustainable water practices. More emphasis is needed to change business and citizen attitudes towards water conservation. These combined efforts aim to create a resilient water future by addressing immediate and long-term conservation needs.

▲▲▲▲▲

Las Cruces offers an exceptional health-focused lifestyle thanks to its warm, sunny climate and high desert environment. With almost three hundred days of sunshine a year, residents have many opportunities for outdoor activities that support physical and mental wellness.

Las Cruces' dry climate also promotes respiratory health, as allergens are lower than in more humid regions. This aspect, combined with the city's numerous wellness and fitness centers, creates a supportive environment for individuals of all ages to prioritize their health.

The mild winters and low humidity make it easy to enjoy outdoor pursuits year-round, including hiking, cycling, and running. The nearby Organ Mountains and numerous trailheads provide scenic, natural backdrops for these activities, allowing people to enjoy both fitness and the mental health benefits of being in nature.

The elevation of Las Cruces, 3,900 feet above sea level, also offers a natural boost for cardiovascular fitness, as the higher altitude helps increase lung capacity over time.

The region's climate is ideal for local farmers' markets, which flourish year-round and provide fresh, locally grown produce. Access to fruits, vegetables, and other organic products contributes to a health-conscious community and fosters a farm-to-table culture. The local cuisine often features green or red chiles and other produce that add flavor and nutrition to meals, reflecting a Southwest-inspired approach to healthy eating.

The combination of abundant sunny days, accessible outdoor spaces, and fresh local produce makes Las Cruces an ideal destination for anyone seeking a healthy lifestyle.

▲▲▲▲▲

The Thomas Branigan Library plays a vital role in enhancing the lifestyle of Las Cruces's citizens. The city's primary public library serves as a knowledge repository and community hub, providing resources, services, and programs catering to its diverse population.

The library offers an extensive collection of books, audiobooks, e-books, and multimedia materials, serving patrons of all ages and interests. The library's collection supports lifelong learning and recreational engagement, whether you're seeking academic resources, leisure reading, or local history.

In addition to traditional library services, the Thomas Branigan Library hosts a variety of educational and cultural programs throughout the year. These include literacy workshops, art exhibits, and after-school programs, contributing to the community's intellectual and cultural enrichment. The library also provides meeting spaces for local organizations, fostering a sense of connection and collaboration among residents.

For those who need assistance with digital literacy or access to technology, the library offers computer workstations, free Wi-Fi, and technology workshops to help bridge the digital divide. This is especially important for individuals needing access to the internet or technology at home, helping them stay connected and informed.

The library's role extends beyond information and technology access. It actively participates in community development and well-being. With programs designed for all ages—from early literacy initiatives for young children to job search resources for adults—the library ensures every community member has opportunities for personal growth and success.

The Thomas Branigan Library is not just a building filled with books but a cornerstone of Las Cruces' civic life. It provides a welcoming environment where residents can learn, connect, and grow, significantly contributing to the city's overall quality of life.

The Friends of the Thomas Branigan Library is a nonprofit organization dedicated to enriching the cultural fabric of our community. Through their support, local authors are given a unique platform to connect with residents, sharing their books, writing processes, and valuable insights. This initiative highlights the diversity and creativity of regional voices and fosters a love for literature and lifelong learning.

In addition to hosting author talks and workshops, the Friends organize community events, fundraisers, and book drives to support library programs and resources. Creating spaces for meaningful dialogue between authors and readers cultivates a sense of connection and inspiration, encouraging aspiring writers to pursue their dreams.

Whether you're a published author or simply a lover of books, The Friends of the Thomas Branigan Library invites you to join them in celebrating the transformative power of storytelling.

▲▲▲▲▲

Dona Ana Community College is a crucial stepping stone to higher education, providing students with the knowledge, skills, and resources they need to succeed academically and professionally. It offers various associate degree programs, certificates, and workforce development opportunities, making higher education accessible and affordable for all learners.

Whether students are looking to transfer to a four-year university, enter the workforce immediately, or gain specialized technical skills, Dona Ana Community College's flexible learning options, including online courses and evening classes, allow them to balance their education with personal and professional commitments. The college offers a supportive environment with small classes, experienced faculty, and various student services, including tutoring, career counseling, and financial aid.

Through strong partnerships with local industries and New Mexico State University, Dona Ana Community College provides students with valuable real-world experience and seamless pathways to continue their education or start their careers. With an emphasis on academic excellence, community engagement, and workforce readiness, the community college is dedicated to helping students achieve their goals and build a brighter future.

In addition to its academic offerings, Dona Ana Community College fosters an active campus community, promoting student involvement through clubs, organizations, and extracurricular activities. This holistic approach to education empowers students to pursue their academic goals, develop leadership skills, and connect with peers, enhancing their overall college experience.

Spaceport America is fifty-five miles north of Las Cruces and is the world's first commercial spaceport designed and constructed for commercial space flight. Built on 18,000 acres of land in the Jornada del Muerto desert basin, the spaceport is adjacent to the U.S. Army's White Sands Missile

Range and under 6,000 square miles of protected airspace.

Spaceport America has FAA-licensed horizontal and vertical launch areas that attract innovative entrepreneurial tenants, including some of the most well-respected companies in the commercial space industry: anchor tenant Virgin Galactic, UP Aerospace, HAPS Mobile, AeroVironment, Spin Launch, and more.

On May 10, 2019, Sir Richard Branson announced that Virgin Galactic would move its California operations to Spaceport America over the coming summer in preparation for the world's first commercial space flights.

New Mexico delivered on its promise to build a world-first and world-class spaceport," Branson said. "Today, I could not be more excited to announce that, in return, we are now ready to bring New Mexico a world-first, world-class space line. Virgin Galactic is coming home to New Mexico, where we will open space to change the world for good together.

Although tenant operations remain private, public tours of the spaceport grounds are offered. Final Frontier Tours departs from Visit Las Cruces at 336 South Main Street. Tour guides provide a site background, and visitors can experience the G-Shock simulator and see the runway to space—all in the beautiful high desert of southern New Mexico. All tours must be booked in advance.

The Bataan Memorial Death March occurs each March. Since its inception, it has grown from about one hundred participants to between eight and ten thousand. Participants come from across the United States and several foreign countries; it has become one of the top marathons in the world and a ceremonial tribute like no other.

On April 9, 1942, 75,000 American and Filipino prisoners of war were forced to march sixty-three miles to an internment camp on the Bataan peninsula by the Imperial Japanese Army.

During that campaign, over 21,000 soldiers lost their lives due to malnutrition, disease, heat exhaustion, and severe physical abuse. Seven decades after the Bataan March, this event brings awareness to the sacrifices made by those brave soldiers.

The bustling Las Cruces Farmers & Crafts Market offers an array of locally grown fruits, vegetables, and artisanal goods, fostering a connection to sustainable, healthy eating. The skills of local craftsmen are also on display.

Whether you're soaking up the sun on a nature excursion or savoring farm-to-table cuisine, Las Cruces offers the perfect environment for embracing wellness and balance. With its serene landscapes and commitment to sustainable living, this vibrant city sets the stage for the next phase of development—one where wellness, innovation, and community thrive together. As the area continues to grow, new opportunities for holistic health, eco-conscious living, and technological advancement will emerge, further enhancing the quality of life for residents and visitors alike.

Las Cruces is not just a place to visit; it's a place to grow, recharge, and be inspired by what's to come. Nestled in the heart of southern New Mexico, this city offers a unique blend of natural beauty, rich cultural heritage, and a thriving community welcoming newcomers and longtime residents alike.

You don't just find yourself; you uncover a deeper understanding of who you are. In doing so, you see a path forward illuminated with opportunities, growth, and endless possibilities for what's next. This journey isn't just about discovering your strengths and passions; it's about embracing challenges, learning from them, and evolving into the version of yourself you've always hoped to become.

Every step you take opens new doors, each one leading to more significant potential, fulfillment, and the chance to shape a future that reflects your true purpose. The road ahead is not always clear, but with each forward move, the horizon broadens, offering a world of endless potential to explore.

Attracting AI-driven companies requires overcoming challenges such as competition from larger cities, the need for skilled workers, and ensuring equitable access to new opportunities. New Mexico State University leads AI research and education today, attracting students and researchers interested in AI applications. The university's focus on AI programs and partnerships with local businesses is producing a tech-savvy workforce, preparing residents for future job opportunities in AI-driven fields.

CHAPTER THREE

Continuing to Change

Las Cruces continues to embrace the digital age; there is a strong focus on sustainability, innovation, and inclusion. The city is exploring further advancements in renewable energy integration, smart agriculture, and virtual public services.

With its expanding tech infrastructure and supportive community, Las Cruces is well-positioned to be a regional leader in technology and innovation in the coming years, balancing growth with a commitment to accessibility and quality of life for all its residents.

The growth of sectors beyond agriculture, such as education, healthcare, and retail, represents a significant shift in many economies worldwide. As the city industrializes and urbanizes, these sectors have become vital contributors to employment, economic development, and societal well-being. An expanded look at these sectors and their transformative impacts are explained.

The education sector has grown tremendously as Las Cruces leaders recognize the importance of a well-educated workforce in a knowledge-driven economy. Investment in primary, secondary, and higher education has increased, alongside vocational and technical training, to meet the demands of various industries.

Digital learning platforms and online education have expanded access to knowledge, especially for the underserved population. With education at the forefront of economic growth, governments and private organizations continue to innovate in this sector to improve literacy rates, skill acquisition, and critical thinking, fueling growth in other sectors like technology, engineering, and healthcare.

As life expectancy rises and medical advancements continue, healthcare has emerged as a dominant sector in employment and innovation. This growth is partly driven by an aging population in many developed nations and increased healthcare access in emerging economies. Healthcare includes hospitals, clinics, pharmaceuticals, biotechnology, mental health services, and a rising wellness industry focused on preventive care.

Technological advancements, such as telemedicine, artificial intelligence in diagnostics, and personalized medicine, are revolutionizing healthcare delivery and making quality care more accessible. Additionally, healthcare now includes a more significant focus on mental health, reflecting a growing awareness of the importance of holistic health for overall societal productivity.

The retail sector has evolved from traditional storefronts to a robust ecosystem that includes e-commerce, mobile shopping, and direct-to-consumer brands. This growth is fueled by rising consumer demand, changing lifestyle patterns, and the internet's global reach. E-commerce giants have transformed the landscape, allowing consumers to shop for products from around the world with the click of a button.

Sustainable and socially responsible retail practices are gaining traction as consumers demand brand transparency and ethical practices. Retail also plays a crucial role in job creation, with millions employed in logistics, customer service, and sales roles. Furthermore, the sector's adaptation to technology, like cashless payments, personalized shopping experiences, and data-driven marketing, underscores its resilience and innovation.

Las Cruces, New Mexico, continues to emerge as a hub for innovation, culture, and community-driven growth. Several key trends are shaping its future, drawing attention to the integration of technology, social responsibility, and globalization.

The city is witnessing a surge in technological advancements transforming local industries. From agricultural tech supporting New Mexico's rich farming heritage to innovations in renewable energy, Las Cruces is becoming a focal point for sustainable technology solutions. New startups and collaborations with New Mexico State

University drive research and development, particularly in drone technology, precision farming, and solar energy. Public initiatives also emphasize smart city infrastructure, with projects to improve transportation, energy efficiency, and public safety.

Las Cruces' community-driven ethos is fostering a strong culture of social responsibility. Local organizations and businesses increasingly adopt practices prioritizing environmental sustainability and community well-being. Efforts such as promoting water conservation, supporting local artisans, and organizing inclusive cultural events are gaining momentum. Nonprofits and grassroots movements are addressing issues like affordable housing and education, ensuring that growth benefits all residents.

Global connections are becoming more evident in Las Cruces, thanks to its strategic location near the U.S.-Mexico border. Cross-border trade and cultural exchange enrich the city's economic and social fabric. The burgeoning international student population at New Mexico State University also contributes to a more global perspective. Businesses are tapping into international markets, while local cuisine, arts, and festivals reflect the blending of diverse influences.

The future of Las Cruces lies in its ability to balance these interconnected trends. It will be crucial to embrace technology while maintaining a commitment to social responsibility and fostering global ties. Collaborative efforts between government, academia, and private enterprises will likely play a key role in navigating this complex landscape. With a focus on innovation and inclusivity, Las Cruces is poised to become a model city that thrives on the synergy of tradition and progress.

Technology drives efficiency and innovations across all sectors, from intelligent classrooms and telemedicine to AI-powered retail insights.

Consumers increasingly value sustainability, pushing these sectors to adopt greener practices through clean energy in healthcare facilities, ethical sourcing in retail, or environmentally friendly school infrastructure.

With globalization, there's a push toward making education, healthcare, and retail services more accessible, especially to underserved populations in rural or remote areas.

These sectors have collectively become major employers, supporting local livelihood and contributing significantly to growth. The shift beyond agriculture highlights an economic evolution in which education, healthcare, and retail are central to a modern economy's resilience, innovation, and sustainability.

Each sector fulfills a unique societal role and synergistically supports the others, building a comprehensive framework for future economic stability and growth.

CHAPTER FOUR

Seeds of Tradition

The transition from agrarian to a mixed economy, combined with urban sprawl and changes in land use, was pressuring traditional farming areas, leading to complex social, environmental, and economic challenges. Expanding developments into previously rural agricultural zones disrupt farming practices that have often existed for generations. This process, sometimes called "land conversion," involves transforming farmland and natural landscapes into urban areas, making way for residential, commercial, and industrial growth.

The causes of urban sprawl in Las Cruces were many and varied. Urban sprawl was primarily driven by population growth and a demand for housing, especially in suburban and exurban areas. As Las Cruces expanded, real estate developers sought land, often cheaper, on the outskirts of cities, where farming land is most abundant. Economic incentives, such as lower property taxes in these areas, encourage developers and buyers alike to consider these once-rural locations. Additionally, advancements in transportation infrastructure made it easier for people to commute from distant suburbs into Las Cruces, further promoting suburbanization.

Citizens have been concerned about the impact on traditional farming areas. As more agricultural land was converted for urban use, farmers were forced to sell their land or adapt to a smaller scale of operation. This loss reduces the land available for local food production and increases reliance on imported food, which has environmental and economic implications.

As urbanization reaches rural areas, land prices typically rise due to speculative purchasing by developers. This can make it difficult for existing farmers to afford additional land for expansion or keep their current operations viable. Young or new farmers, in particular, face challenges in securing affordable land, which limits their ability to enter or sustain careers in agriculture.

The transformation of farmland into urban landscapes disrupts ecosystems, affecting soil health, water availability, and biodiversity. Urbanization often increases the runoff of pollutants into nearby waterways, affecting both the immediate area and downstream agricultural lands. Traditional farming practices that rely on natural resources are frequently hampered by reduced water availability and soil degradation caused by urban activities.

Urban populations' proximity to farmland can pressure farmers to adopt different practices. For instance, organic farming and agritourism are becoming more popular as farms near urban centers try to adapt to consumer demand. However, these changes can be costly and require significant adaptation for traditional farmers.

Additionally, farms may face restrictions on specific activities, such as operating heavy machinery during early morning or late-night hours, applying pesticides near residential areas, or engaging in practices that generate excessive noise or dust. These limitations often arise from concerns voiced by nearby residents about health, safety, and overall quality of life, compelling farms to adopt more community-conscious and environmentally friendly approaches.

As urban areas encroach upon farming communities, there is often a cultural shift as well. Farmers are surrounded by non-farming neighbors who may not understand or appreciate agricultural practices, leading to noise, odor, and dust conflicts. The influx of urban residents can also change the social fabric of rural areas as long-standing agricultural communities are replaced or mixed with suburban newcomers.

There have been attempts to mitigate the impacts of urban sprawl. Several strategies help reduce the effects of urban sprawl on traditional farming areas. Zoning laws and land-use regulations are essential tools that local governments can use to protect farmland by restricting urban development in designated agricultural zones. Conservation easements allow farmers to sell development rights to their land, ensuring that it remains dedicated to agriculture even if it changes ownership.

Educational research has influenced the growth and development of Las Cruces. New Mexico State University has significantly expanded its academic and research footprint, evolving into a pivotal institution that drives innovation in biotechnology, renewable energy, and computer science.

Its commitment to high-impact research has attracted top-tier faculty, fostered collaborative partnerships with government agencies, and created valuable opportunities for students to engage in innovative projects.

In biotechnology, New Mexico State University has emerged as a leader in agricultural advancements and health sciences, pivotal in addressing challenges unique to the Southwest region. The university's research focuses on critical issues such as developing drought-resistant crops, innovative pest management strategies, and livestock improvement to enhance food security and sustainability in the region's arid climate. NMSU's biotechnology programs emphasize cutting-edge genetic research, precision agriculture technologies, and sustainable farming practices to help local communities and farmers adapt to changing environmental conditions.

Furthermore, the university is advancing health sciences by exploring new biotechnological approaches to improve human and animal health, particularly in underserved rural areas. Through collaborations with industry partners, government agencies, and global research networks, New Mexico State University continues to drive innovation and foster economic growth in the Southwest, making significant contributions to agricultural sustainability and healthcare advancements.

Through its Agricultural Science Center, researchers work on enhancing crop yield and quality, addressing water scarcity challenges, and developing sustainable farming practices that support local economies and improve food security.

The university's groundbreaking renewable energy research emphasizes solar, wind, and geothermal technologies tailored to New Mexico's unique climate. New Mexico State University's Center for Renewable Energy and Sustainability Research is a hub for innovations in energy storage, innovative grid technologies, and sustainable energy solutions.

Students and faculty collaborate closely to design and refine innovative, scalable energy models that aim to transform energy usage in urban and rural communities. These models are tailored to reduce reliance on fossil fuels, integrate renewable energy sources, and improve overall energy efficiency. Participants explore cutting-edge technologies such as solar panels, wind turbines, energy storage systems, and smart grids through interdisciplinary teamwork.

The initiative focuses on technical solutions and incorporates socioeconomic factors to ensure the models are accessible, affordable, and adaptable to diverse community needs. Students gain hands-on experience conducting energy audits, analyzing data, and working with stakeholders to implement sustainable practices. Faculty members bring engineering, environmental science, and economics expertise to guide research and development, fostering an environment of innovation and collaboration.

In addition to reducing carbon footprints, the program emphasizes community engagement through workshops, training programs, and partnerships with local organizations. Addressing the unique challenges different regions face contributes to a cleaner, more resilient environment while empowering communities to take charge of their energy futures.

In computer science, New Mexico State University has made significant strides in cybersecurity, artificial intelligence, and data analytics. The Department collaborates with tech industry leaders to prepare students for software engineering, AI development, and data science careers. By focusing on cybersecurity, New Mexico State University aims to address critical issues in digital safety and privacy, preparing a new generation of experts capable of tackling the complexities of an increasingly digital world.

With state-of-the-art labs, funding from major organizations, and a commitment to serving academic and local communities, New Mexico State University's expansion has positioned it as a cornerstone of research and education in the Southwest. It influences the local economy and contributes valuable insights and innovations to global scientific challenges.

Small business growth has enhanced the local economy, and a notable rise in small businesses supporting and strengthening the agricultural sector has been seen. New ventures focused on food processing, craft breweries, and regional markets are gaining traction, each contributing to a sustainable food ecosystem. Local food processors transform raw agricultural products into high-quality goods catering to residents and nearby communities, creating jobs and bolstering the local economy.

Craft breweries, often sourcing ingredients like hops, barley, and seasonal fruits from local farms, appeal to craft beer enthusiasts and foster a sense of community pride in regional flavors.

Additionally, regional markets have become popular gathering spots where small-scale farmers, artisans, and food producers display fresh produce, handmade products, and locally sourced goods. This constructive interaction between agriculture and small business fuels economic growth and strengthens community connections, paving the way for a resilient and diverse local economy.

Other approaches involve incentivizing urban density rather than expansion, encouraging developers to make better use of existing urban space. Public awareness and policy advocacy are also critical, enabling communities to recognize the value of preserving agricultural land. Lastly, expanding support for urban and community-supported agriculture (programs can significantly enhance the integration of farming into urban environments, creating a bridge between city dwellers and local food production.

These initiatives provide access to fresh, locally grown produce and offer educational opportunities that foster awareness about sustainable agricultural practices. Urban gardens, rooftop farms, and Community-supported agriculture partnerships can transform unused urban spaces into productive hubs, promoting environmental stewardship, reducing food miles, and strengthening community bonds.

By fostering these connections, urban agriculture becomes a powerful tool for cultivating a deeper appreciation for the origins of food and the importance of sustainable living in densely populated areas.

Urban sprawl presents ongoing challenges for traditional farming areas, from economic pressures to environmental impacts. Addressing these requires thoughtful planning, policy intervention, and community engagement to balance urban growth and the preservation of vital agricultural land.

Las Cruces today is a knowledge and innovation hub for the Southwest. It has emerged as a knowledge-based economy driven by substantial contributions to research, higher education, and a thriving tech startup scene.

The university is considering adopting the Community Education model as a strategic approach to enhance the quality of life for its citizens. This model aims to actively engage the entire community in processes that lead to meaningful, sustainable improvements. Community Education is not just a program but a comprehensive process and philosophy that focuses on delivering educational and human services that ensure equal access to information and opportunities for all individuals.

At its core, Community Education emphasizes the empowerment of local citizens by fostering a collaborative environment where diverse voices are heard, valued, and incorporated into decision-making. It is driven by regular and ongoing input from various community members, including residents, local organizations, and stakeholders. This participatory approach allows for identifying community needs and priorities, ensuring that educational programs and services are relevant, inclusive, and responsive to the specific challenges faced by the community.

By integrating educational initiatives with community development efforts, the model encourages lifelong learning, enhances social cohesion, and promotes civic engagement. The university's commitment to this model is rooted in the belief that fostering a well-educated and informed community is vital to creating a thriving, equitable society where all individuals can succeed.

The university aims to create a platform that supports collaborative learning, skill-building, and access to resources directly impacting the community's well-being. Through this approach, Community Education can become a powerful tool for social change, fostering stronger relationships and creating a more inclusive future for all citizens.

The university is considering using the Community Education model to encourage the use of all the community to improve the quality of life for its citizens effectively. Community Education is a process, a philosophy, and a program designed to deliver human and educational services with equal access to information. It is fueled by ongoing and regular input from various community members.

The tech startup ecosystem in Las Cruces has flourished, bolstered by collaborative workspaces, local incubators, and initiatives to support small businesses. Programs like Arrowhead Center, a New Mexico State University business incubator, provide essential resources, mentorship, and funding opportunities for new ventures. This support has catalyzed the growth of startups in sectors such as renewable energy, aerospace, cybersecurity, and agro-tech, drawing a mix of young talent and experienced professionals to the region.

Las Cruces's commitment to education has further reinforced its role as an innovation hub. In addition to New Mexico State University, other institutions and training programs prepare a skilled workforce aligned with regional industries. The city's focus on sustainability and community-driven development projects underscores its role as a forward-thinking hub of knowledge and technological advancement in the Southwest.

Several vital institutions are significantly shaping Las Cruces's economic landscape, with New Mexico State University, White Sands Missile Range, Spaceport America, and local government efforts playing central roles. They are vital economic powerhouses in the region. One of the largest military installations in the United States, it spans over 3,200 square miles across southern New Mexico. This vast expanse of desert serves as a premier testing site for rockets, missiles, and other defense technologies, playing a critical role in national security and innovation.

The missile range provides thousands of jobs, directly employing military personnel, government contractors, and civilian staff. It also supports local economies by creating opportunities for businesses that supply goods and services to the installation. Additionally, the federal funding attracted by the range significantly benefits surrounding communities, contributing to infrastructure projects, educational initiatives, and community development programs.

White Sands Missile Range and Spaceport America also draw scientific and technological talent to the region, fostering partnerships with universities, research institutions, and private companies. Its testing facilities have hosted groundbreaking experiments, including the first atomic bomb test, code-named "Trinity," in 1945. It continues to be a hub for cutting-edge aerospace and defense research.

Beyond their economic and strategic significance, both contribute to the area's cultural and historical fabric. Visitors can explore the area's history through the White Sands Missile Range Museum, which showcases artifacts, exhibits, and stories highlighting its role in shaping modern technology and defense.

With its economic impact, strategic importance, and historical relevance, the White Sands Missile Range and Spaceport America remain a cornerstone of the region's identity and a catalyst for future growth and innovation.

The installation's role in testing innovative defense technologies attracts contractors and suppliers, leading to business opportunities for local companies. White Sands Missile Range's presence has also catalyzed partnerships with educational institutions like New Mexico State University, aligning the skills of the local workforce with the needs of the defense industry.

Additionally, the base's demand for goods and services—from construction to maintenance—supports many local businesses, making White

Sands Missile Range a cornerstone of economic stability in the region.

Local Governments have implemented policies and initiatives to sustain and expand the economic opportunities these institutions provide. They work to attract and retain businesses through incentives, investments in infrastructure, and partnerships with New Mexico State University and White Sands Missile Range.

Programs focused on supporting small businesses, streamlining permitting processes, and encouraging tourism contribute to economic diversification. Additionally, local government initiatives in housing, transportation, and public safety create a solid foundation that benefits residents and institutions like New Mexico State University and White Sands Missile Range, helping foster a stable economic environment conducive to growth.

New Mexico State University is a hub of educational research and workforce development, equipping students with the skills to thrive in various industries. Its research initiatives, particularly in agriculture, energy, and aerospace, attract significant federal and private funding, while its collaboration with local businesses spurs entrepreneurship and technological advancements.

White Sands Missile Range, a cornerstone of defense and technology innovation, brings the region high-paying jobs and advanced technological infrastructure. Its testing facilities and partnerships with private defense contractors ensure that New Mexico remains a critical player in national security and advancing cutting-edge technologies.

Meanwhile, local government provides essential infrastructure, policy support, and incentives that encourage business growth and attract diverse industries to the area. By fostering a business-friendly environment and investing in community development, local authorities create the conditions necessary for sustained economic prosperity.

This triad anchors the city's economy and drives diversification, helping Las Cruces remain competitive amid shifts in industries such as renewable energy, aerospace, and technology. Together, these institutions form a dynamic and synergistic partnership that effectively balances the time-honored traditions of their respective fields with the forward-thinking spirit of innovation. This harmonious collaboration preserves economic stability and drives sustainable growth, ensuring resilience in changing global markets.

Blending established practices with cutting-edge advancements creates fertile ground for exploring new opportunities and fosters a robust foundation for future generations.

This partnership catalyzes progress, setting the stage for transformative change and opening new avenues for success and prosperity.

Leveraging each partner's strengths and expertise fosters innovation, encourages collaboration, and drives sustainable growth. Together, they can tackle complex challenges, adapt to evolving market dynamics, and unlock untapped potential. This alliance paves the way for immediate success. It lays a solid foundation for long-term impact, positioning both parties at the forefront of industry advancements and shaping the future of their respective fields.

Through its Agricultural Extension Service, New Mexico State University supports local agriculture, helping farmers and ranchers implement sustainable practices that improve productivity and contribute to the economy. Research initiatives at New Mexico State University, especially those in aerospace, environmental science, and renewable energy, often lead to collaborations with private companies, generating jobs, attracting grants, and fostering entrepreneurship.

New Mexico State University will significantly drive the region's economic growth and workforce development. Its agriculture, engineering, and technology programs are essential for preparing skilled workers and innovators.

The university's focus on research and education helps keep the area competitive, with New Mexico State University graduates entering diverse fields that support local industries.

CHAPTER FIVE

Prospects

The future of agriculture lies in seamlessly integrating advanced technology with sustainable practices, creating growth opportunities that benefit both farmers and the environment. By adopting precision farming techniques, such as drone monitoring for pest control, soil sensors for optimizing water use, and data analytics for tracking crop health, farmers can make informed decisions that reduce resource waste, increase efficiency, and improve yields. These technologies help minimize the environmental footprint by conserving water, reducing pesticide use, and improving soil health, making agriculture more resilient to climate challenges. However, overcoming barriers like technology costs and access to training will ensure that all farmers can benefit from these innovations. Furthermore, integrating new technologies with traditional farming practices will provide a balanced, sustainable approach to the future of agriculture.

With advancements in agro-tech, from vertical farming systems to automated irrigation and AI-driven crop management, the potential for transformative agricultural practices has never been more significant. As technology continues to evolve, so does the capacity for intelligent farming solutions that can cater to various scales of agriculture, from large commercial operations to small family-owned farms.

Sustainable growth will require collaboration across sectors, including government, private industries, and local communities. Policy support, investment in agro-tech startups, and educational programs to empower farmers with the skills to use modern technologies will be crucial for scaling sustainable practices.

The agricultural industry is well-positioned as a cornerstone for a sustainable global economy. By integrating environmental stewardship with productivity, agriculture can contribute to food security, job creation, and preserving natural resources for future generations. This balance between economic growth and ecological integrity will be essential for the industry's ongoing success and relevance in an increasingly eco-conscious world.

Managing resources, urban expansion, and balancing heritage with innovation is challenging but provides opportunities. Las Cruces faces the critical challenge of balancing growth with sustainability in today's fast-paced world. Rapid urban expansion and population growth put significant pressure on natural resources, from water and energy to green spaces and waste management.

The city planners and officials must prioritize sustainable resource management by adopting green practices that benefit both the environment and the community. This includes investing in renewable energy sources such as solar and wind power to reduce reliance on fossil fuels and mitigate the effects of climate change. Implementing efficient public transportation systems can reduce traffic congestion, lower carbon emissions, and make commuting more accessible for residents. Eco-friendly waste management systems, such as recycling programs and composting initiatives, help minimize landfill use and promote resource conservation.

Furthermore, integrating green spaces, sustainable building designs, and water conservation practices can enhance the urban environment, improving residents' quality of life. These efforts support the environment and foster a more livable, resilient Las Cruces where people and nature thrive together. The city will ensure long-term prosperity and a healthier future by prioritizing sustainability.

Preserving heritage and local culture is essential in fostering community identity. As the city expands, historical sites and cultural landmarks risk being overshadowed or even replaced by new developments.

This challenge presents an opportunity to integrate heritage into modern spaces creatively, blending historical preservation with contemporary architecture and urban design. It involves restoring old buildings, repurposing business and industrial areas, and creating public spaces that will bridge the past and future, enriching cityscapes with layers of meaning.

Innovation and technology offer vast potential for addressing urban challenges and transforming Las Cruces into a more efficient, sustainable, and livable space. Integrating innovative city technologies, such as smart infrastructure, devices, and AI-powered systems, can significantly improve urban management. Data-driven decision-making, powered by real-time analytics and machine learning, allows city planners to anticipate issues, optimize resources, and improve service delivery.

For example, AI-powered platforms assist doctors in interpreting medical images more accurately and providing predictive analytics to guide treatment plans. Moreover, AI-driven virtual consultations can make healthcare more accessible by allowing patients to receive care remotely, which is especially beneficial in areas with limited healthcare infrastructure.

Collaborations with local tech companies and startups can bring fresh ideas, cutting-edge solutions, and expertise, enabling the city to experiment with new approaches to complex challenges like traffic congestion, waste management, energy consumption, and public safety. Smart grids, autonomous transportation systems, and digital platforms for community engagement are just a few examples of how technology can help streamline city services, reduce costs, and enhance the quality of life for residents.

Moreover, technological innovation supports sustainability goals by making the city more energy-efficient, resilient to climate change, and environmentally friendly. In addition to improving the city infrastructure, these technologies will drive inclusivity and equity by ensuring that all residents have access to the benefits of modern urban services.

Overall, Las Cruces's future hinges on its ability to leverage innovation and technology to create more efficient, adaptable, and sustainable environments that meet the evolving needs of its diverse and growing population. By embracing smart infrastructure, investing in cutting-edge technologies, and fostering a culture of innovation, the city can enhance its quality of life, drive economic growth, and address critical challenges such as urban sprawl, energy efficiency, and climate resilience.

Integrating transportation, healthcare, education, and public services systems will improve residents' daily lives and position Las Cruces as a model for modern, future-ready cities. Through collaboration with tech companies, universities, and community stakeholders, Las Cruces can build a thriving, forward-thinking city that is well-prepared for tomorrow's demands.

The challenge lies in implementing these technologies equitably, ensuring they benefit all communities, especially underserved areas, and do not contribute to social divides.

Las Cruces will redefine urban life through sustainable development, cultural preservation, and inclusive innovation. With careful planning, it will become a sustainable, tech-forward hub that celebrates heritage while supporting future generations.

Las Cruces is known for its warm community spirit, local culture, and numerous contributions from its residents. Here are some key ways the city's good citizens make it a welcoming and wonderful place to live.

Las Cruces residents take pride in their small businesses, helping to cultivate a unique local economy. Locals actively support and celebrate homegrown talent, from cafes like Muddy River Coffee Shop, where cats and coffee combine for a cozy atmosphere, to local artisans who display their crafts at the Las Cruces Farmers and Crafts Market. The community's appreciation for the arts is also evident in public events like Art Forms for the Love of Art Month, which turns the entire city into an art gallery every February.

Promoting outdoor activities and environmental stewardship with its striking desert landscapes and proximity to the Organ Mountains, Las Cruces offers many opportunities for outdoor recreation. Local groups often organize hiking, biking, and nature walks, fostering a shared respect for the land. Community-driven conservation efforts, such as Keep Las Cruces Beautiful, aim to preserve local trails and parks, instilling a sense of environmental responsibility.

New Mexico State University is a hub for education and research, offering various community outreach programs and lectures open to the public. Libraries and community centers regularly host workshops and literacy programs, ensuring everyone can access lifelong learning opportunities. This focus on education contributes to an informed, engaged, and initiative-taking community.

A dedicated network of local volunteers supports organizations like Casa de Peregrinos, which provides food assistance to those in need, and Mesilla Valley Community of Hope, a center for the homeless. Community-driven initiatives like toy and food drives, holiday assistance programs, and shelters for people and animals highlight the residents' compassion and commitment to supporting vulnerable community members.

Neighborhood associations work with local law enforcement to ensure a secure environment. At the same time, community events, like Movies in the Park and the Downtown Ramble, offer safe, enjoyable, and family-friendly activities. The citizens' active involvement in community safety programs helps maintain a sense of security for all residents.

Las Cruces citizens take pride in promoting sustainability and environmental responsibility. Initiatives like solar energy projects and water conservation programs are popular among residents, and the city's farmers' market is a model for sustainable agriculture and support for local food producers. This focus on green initiatives demonstrates a collective commitment to fostering a healthier and more sustainable environment for future generations.

By prioritizing eco-friendly practices, we reduce our carbon footprint, preserve natural resources, improve air and water quality, and combat climate change. These efforts are crucial for our planet's and its inhabitants' well-being. As we transition towards more sustainable energy sources, reduce waste, and promote conservation, we lay the groundwork for a more resilient and equitable future. This shared responsibility to protect the environment underscores the importance of collaboration across communities, industries, and governments to ensure we leave a thriving world for generations.

Through these and countless other actions, the people of Las Cruces create a city that is more than just a place to live—a nurturing community that cares deeply for its history, future, and every individual who calls it home. From preserving its rich cultural heritage to embracing innovative growth, Las Cruces is a city where the past and future coexist harmoniously. Residents work together to foster inclusivity, compassion, and resilience, creating a supportive environment where everyone feels valued.

Whether through local arts initiatives, volunteerism, or a commitment to sustainable development, community spirit is woven into everyday life's fabric. Las Cruces is not just a city— it's a collective journey, a living testament to the resilience and spirit of its people. Every individual, every family, and every community group contributes to the fabric of this place, playing a vital role in shaping a thriving, connected, and hopeful future. With its rich cultural heritage, diverse population, and commitment to progress, Las Cruces stands as a leader of possibility in the heart of the Southwest.

Collaboration is the cornerstone of success — whether it's local businesses, educational institutions, or neighbors working together to create lasting change. Las Cruces is more than just a home; it's a vision for a future where everyone is empowered to contribute, and every voice is heard.

In Las Cruces, hope is an ideal and a way of life. It's seen in how people lift each other, celebrate diversity, and face challenges with determination. The city is a community that believes in the power of unity and the importance of building a sustainable future for generations to come. Through creativity, hard work, and compassion, Las Cruces is transforming into a city where opportunity, connection, and hope are within reach for all.

CHAPTER SIX

Vision for Las Cruces's Future

Las Cruces will continue to evolve as a dynamic and thriving region where its agricultural roots blend seamlessly with cutting-edge technological advancements. This vision embraces the area's rich agricultural heritage while fostering growth in renewable energy, innovation, and technology.

The significance of AI to Las Cruces's future will lie in its potential to transform multiple sectors, boost local innovation, and improve residents' quality of life. As AI technologies advance, the city could benefit in several key areas—a robust agricultural presence, helping farmers optimize water usage, crop health monitoring, and pest control. AI-driven data analysis could support sustainable farming practices, essential in a region where water conservation is critical.

AI will transform healthcare in Las Cruces by improving diagnostic accuracy, enhancing patient care workflows, and expanding access to services. For rural and underserved populations surrounding the city, AI-driven telemedicine and diagnostic tools can bridge the gap in access to specialized care, enabling more timely diagnoses and treatment.

However, addressing challenges such as internet connectivity and data privacy concerns are essential to ensure equitable adoption while involving local healthcare providers in the implementation process.

Las Cruces will use AI to optimize public services, from traffic management to energy efficiency. It will improve infrastructure, reduce congestion, and monitor environmental conditions, creating a safer and more efficient urban environment.

Community-focused AI applications, such as safeguarding indigenous languages or creating interactive museum exhibits, will foster a deeper connection to the region's unique heritage. AI significantly enhances Las Cruces' cultural identity by supporting the arts and storytelling and preserving local history through digital projects. These AI-driven initiatives help capture and share the stories, traditions, and cultural practices that define Las Cruces while engaging locals and visitors in meaningful ways. By embracing AI technologies, the community will strengthen its cultural fabric and ensure its rich history is accessible to future generations.

Las Cruces has a unique opportunity to thoughtfully leverage AI, addressing local needs while preserving the city's rich cultural identity and sense of community. By adopting a balanced approach to AI implementation, the city can enhance its sustainability, foster innovation, and build resilience without sacrificing its distinctive character.

Las Cruces could use AI integration for urban planning, where AI-driven data analytics helps optimize resource allocation for infrastructure, transportation, and environmental management. For instance, AI-powered systems reduce energy consumption by improving traffic flow, managing water resources more efficiently, and even predicting maintenance needs for city services. This approach makes Las Cruces more sustainable and sets an example for other mid-sized cities aiming for intelligent growth.

Additionally, AI supports local industries, from agriculture to small businesses. With AI-driven insights, farmers increase crop yield while reducing water usage, helping the agricultural sector adapt to the region's arid climate. Local businesses use AI tools to understand customer preferences and market trends better, giving them a competitive edge without compromising the city's small-town charm.

Las Cruces uses AI to improve public health and safety. Predictive analytics help detect public health risks early, and AI-enhanced emergency response systems ensure faster, more efficient assistance.

The city provides training and resources to ensure community members and local authorities are well-prepared to engage with AI in ways that enhance, rather than overshadow, the human-centered values that define Las Cruces.

AI has the potential to attract tech startup companies to Las Cruces, positioning the city as a regional hub for AI research, innovation, and application. The city could diversify its economy and create a thriving, sustainable ecosystem by strategically investing in AI-driven initiatives, such as creating tech incubators, expanding AI-focused educational programs, and fostering industry partnerships. This would generate high-skilled jobs and drive local businesses' growth through AI adoption, particularly in sectors like agriculture, healthcare, and defense, where AI has the potential to create new opportunities.

The future of Las Cruces will be defined by a harmonious balance between preserving its traditions and embracing the future, creating a sustainable and prosperous community where agriculture, green energy, and technology-driven industries will work together for the benefit of all. This unique blend of time-honored farming practices and cultural legacy paves the way for fresh growth in green technology, sustainable agriculture, local business innovation, and education.

By supporting and cultivating a dynamic ecosystem that matches tradition with innovative solutions, Las Cruces will emerge as a model for other communities striving to balance environmental stewardship, economic development, and social progress. Through partnerships among farmers, entrepreneurs, researchers, and educators, the area will position itself at the forefront of the global movement toward a more sustainable and resilient future.

As Las Cruces nurtures its rich historical foundations while embracing innovative and forward-thinking developments, it is poised to become a community that empowers its residents, attracts visitors, and inspires future generations. By blending its cultural heritage with modern growth, the city will offer a dynamic environment that fosters creativity, economic opportunity, and sustainable progress.

With a focus on enhancing education, preserving natural beauty, and promoting inclusivity, Las Cruces will become a hub for innovation, where diverse communities thrive and everyone can contribute to the city's bright future. Through these efforts, Las Cruces will continue to honor its past while shaping an exciting and prosperous tomorrow.

These influences are honored through historic landmarks, museums, and festivals that foster pride in its unique identity. At the same time, Las Cruces embraces a sustainable, connected, and resilient future with a commitment to renewable energy, green spaces, and innovative urban planning. Initiatives supporting local businesses, arts, and technology enhance economic vitality while strengthening the community bond.

With an emphasis on education and resources for the next generation, Las Cruces will inspire surrounding communities by demonstrating how honoring the past can lay the foundation for an inclusive and forward-thinking future. This approach underscores the importance of preserving cultural heritage while embracing innovation to address the challenges of tomorrow.

A strong commitment to education is at the core of the city's identity. The city focuses on providing resources that empower the next generation to build a brighter, more equitable future. Las Cruces offers many programs to foster knowledge, creativity, and civic responsibility.

These initiatives span the local school district and university, as well as civic organizations and cultural centers, all of which play a vital role in shaping a thriving and interconnected community. Through these efforts, Las Cruces nurtures the growth of its residents and cultivates a spirit of innovation and collaboration.

New Mexico State University will be a pivotal learning, research, and citizen engagement hub. It hosts programs encouraging students to explore diverse fields, from agricultural sciences and environmental sustainability to advanced technology and cultural studies, preparing them for impactful careers that contribute to the broader community.

Beyond formal education, Las Cruces will promote lifelong learning through its libraries, museums, and cultural events. Programs like youth internships and mentorships with local artisans, business leaders, and cultural preservation advocates will create a unique environment where young people can connect with their roots while gaining the skills needed for tomorrow's challenges.

Las Cruces will exemplify how honoring the past can pave the way toward a dynamic and forward-looking future. By valuing diversity, fostering educational opportunities, and nurturing the next generation's potential, the city will illustrate how a powerful sense of community will create a thriving environment where all individuals feel valued and empowered.

This commitment to inclusivity fuels collaboration, innovation, and a shared responsibility to address local challenges. As residents from varied backgrounds bring unique perspectives, the city will become a hub for cultural exchange and growth.

The emphasis on education goes beyond merely transmitting knowledge; it equips young minds with the critical thinking skills, emotional intelligence, and ethical foundations necessary to navigate the world's complexities. Education empowers students to excel academically and become compassionate, initiative-taking leaders by fostering creativity, resilience, and empathy.

Education will be pivotal in shaping a prosperous and interconnected future. It is the foundation upon which residents of Las Cruces will build their potential. It provides the knowledge, skills, and critical thinking abilities necessary for personal growth and societal advancement.

▲▲▲▲▲

Climate change will be a topic of intense local debate. As global temperatures rise and extreme weather events become more frequent, the impact of climate change on Las Cruces will become increasingly evident. The results of this debate and the actions taken—at the national, state, or local level—will have significant consequences for residents, businesses, and the environment.

Like many parts of the Southwest, Las Cruces is already experiencing the effects of climate change in the form of increased temperatures and more frequent droughts. As the debate over climate policy continues, the region will see more extreme weather events, including prolonged heatwaves, wildfires, and flash flooding. These events will disrupt daily life, harm infrastructure, and pose serious risks to public health.

Water is a critical resource in the arid Southwest. Climate change is expected to exacerbate water scarcity in the region, affecting agricultural production, access to drinking water, and energy generation. Las Cruces, which depends on the Rio Grande River for much of its water supply, may face increasing pressure to manage its water resources effectively, leading to stricter regulations and potential conflicts over water usage.

The local economy in Las Cruces is heavily reliant on agriculture, particularly crops like Chile, pecans, and cotton. Climate change threatens crop yields due to water shortages, temperature fluctuations, and the increased risk of pests and diseases. If local farmers cannot adapt to these changes, it will lead to economic loss and job disruptions in the agricultural sector, rippling through the entire community.

Rising temperatures and shifting climate patterns will also exacerbate public health issues. Heat-related illnesses, such as heat strokes, are likely to increase, especially in vulnerable populations like the elderly and low-income communities. Additionally, air quality in Las Cruces may deteriorate due to higher levels of ground-level ozone, which can worsen respiratory conditions like asthma.

The debate on climate change within Las Cruces and beyond will determine how effectively the region responds to these challenges. If local, state, and national leaders embrace bold climate action, Las Cruces could see improvements in renewable energy, energy efficiency, and climate adaptation strategies.

For instance, transitioning to renewable energy sources like solar power could reduce the city's carbon footprint while creating local jobs in the clean energy sector. Improved water management practices and sustainable agricultural techniques could help mitigate the effects of droughts and ensure long-term food security.

On the other hand, if the debate results in insufficient action or policies that delay addressing climate change, Las Cruces could face worsening environmental conditions, economic instability, and more significant public health risks. Residents, businesses, and policymakers must work together to build resilience and adapt to the changing climate.

The outcomes of the climate change debate will significantly shape the future of Las Cruces, with impacts felt across various sectors, from agriculture to public health. The decisions made now, both locally and nationally, will determine how well the city will adapt to the challenges posed by a changing climate, ensuring that future generations can thrive in a more sustainable and resilient community.

AI will potentially attract tech companies and startups, helping to diversify its economy and position it as a regional hub for environmental research and applications. By investing in AI-driven initiatives, such as creating tech incubators, AI-focused ecological programs, and industry partnerships, Las Cruces can foster a thriving ecosystem that generates high-skilled jobs and supports the growth of local businesses.

In an era of rapid technological advancement and cultural exchange, education will be crucial in breaking down barriers, promoting inclusivity, and building bridges between diverse communities. It empowers individuals to adapt to change, innovate, and solve the pressing challenges of our time, such as climate change, inequality, and conflict.

Furthermore, education cultivates a sense of responsibility, not only to oneself but also to the greater good, inspiring individuals to contribute meaningfully to the well-being of their communities. By nurturing the potential of every person, education lays the groundwork for sustainable progress, creating environments where individuals can thrive collectively and contribute to a future characterized by opportunity, harmony, and shared success.

▲▲▲▲▲

The traditions, values, passions, and ideals of María Elena Chávez, Samuel Blake, and Toh-Nah are deeply woven into the fabric of Las Cruces and continue to thrive in the hearts and minds of its citizens. These early visionaries, each contributing unique perspectives and legacies, have shaped the community in ways that remain evident today.

María Elena Chávez, with her deep commitment to cultural preservation and community unity, instilled a lasting respect for heritage and tradition. Her passion for the arts, local customs, and the preservation of language has inspired generations to honor their roots while embracing the future. Her legacy continues in the cultural festivals, the art galleries that showcase local talent, and the educational programs that teach the history of Las Cruces with pride.

Samuel Blake's spirit of innovation and progress also endures in the city. Known for his entrepreneurial mindset and dedication to growth, Blake laid the groundwork for the city's expansion, and his vision for modern infrastructure is still visible in the thriving commercial districts and well-maintained public spaces. His ideals of community development and economic sustainability have left an indelible mark, inspiring local businesses, entrepreneurs, and civic leaders to continue pursuing growth that is both forward-thinking and rooted in responsibility.

Toh-Nah, a pivotal figure in Las Cruces' history, brought the wisdom of indigenous traditions to the community, enriching it with an understanding of balance, respect for nature, and the importance of spiritual connection. His teachings about sustainability and the natural world are especially relevant today as the city continues to promote environmental awareness and conservation efforts. The respect for nature and commitment to preserving Las Cruces' green spaces are a direct tribute to Toh-Nah's influence.

These three prominent figures' traditions, values, and ideals thrive in Las Cruces. From cultural celebrations to business innovation to environmental stewardship, the spirit of María

Elena Chávez, Samuel Blake, and Toh-Nah lives on. Today, many progressive communities contend with individuals like Don Fernando Ortega, who prioritize personal gain over collective well-being. These opportunists often exploit community resources, manipulate systems meant for public benefit, or sidestep ethical obligations in their pursuit of profit.

Their actions, cloaked in the guise of progress or innovation, can create deep divisions, erode trust, and undermine efforts to foster equity and inclusivity. Recognizing and addressing the influence of such individuals is essential to maintaining a community's integrity and ensuring its growth aligns with the common good.

Their legacy is not merely a historical memory but a living tradition woven into Las Cruces' community identity. It is an enduring source of inspiration, motivating the city's citizens to uphold these ideals with pride and dedication. Through cultural events, educational programs, and community initiatives, the people of Las Cruces actively honor and preserve this heritage, ensuring it remains a guiding force for future generations. This shared commitment unites the community and reinforces a sense of purpose and belonging, celebrating the unique spirit of Las Cruces in every endeavor.

THE END

Other books by George Pintar

Fiction

A New Peek at Old West County

Fascinating New Mexico Stories

Musing of an Ostrich Farmer

Navajo Revenge

Never Too Late

The Adventures of Chile Charlie

The Camel's Nose in the Tent

Three Unique Cats

When is it Too Late?

Navajo Tainted Beliefs

Nonfiction

Digging Deeper into Networking

Networking for Profit

The Fundamentals of Grant Writing

Building Stronger Communities

AUTHOR'S NOTES

My bibliography is available on my website, www.georgepintarbooks.com, where readers can explore the complete list of works that define my literary journey. For those interested in learning more about the mysteries behind my unique writing style, the site also provides insights into my creative process, influences, and the themes that run through my books.

Whether you're a long-time fan or a new reader, this is the place to dive deeper into the stories and the mind behind the words. Explore the layers of meaning, the inspiration behind each narrative, and the creative process that brings the characters and worlds to life. Here, you'll find insights into the writing journey, behind-the-scenes details, and a closer look at the themes and messages woven throughout the work. Get ready to unlock new perspectives and discover hidden treasures within the pages.

Here is how you can reach me:

George Pintar
853 Chile Court
Las Cruces, NM 88001
575-680-6515

Made in the USA
Columbia, SC
07 May 2025